Creative
Faith

Creative Faith

Religion as a Way of Worldmaking

Don Cupitt

POLEBRIDGE PRESS
Salem, Oregon

Cover and interior design by Robaire Ream

Library of Congress Cataloging-in-Publication Data
Cupitt, Don.
  Creative faith : religion as a way of worldmaking / by Don Cupitt.
    pages cm
  Includes bibliographical references.
  ISBN 978-1-59815-153-4 (alk. paper)
 1. Humanitarianism. 2. Ethics. 3. Christianity--Influence. 4. Jesus Christ.
I. Title.
  BJ1475.3.C87 2015
  205--dc23
                                                        2014034134

To Lila

Contents

Introduction

t the time of his death at the age of 95 in 2013, Nelson Mandela was perhaps the most highly and widely esteemed person on earth. As the turnout of world leaders at his funeral showed, wherever you stood on the political spectrum you could not but admire the fortitude and the personal integrity of a man who had struggled for so long and amidst such extreme adversity—and then in his later years had triumphed so spectacularly, bringing his country through a major political transformation without bloodshed and becoming its first president.[1]

Naturally the event received vast and worldwide media coverage, and one expected journalists to enquire about the intellectual and moral influences that had formed this exceptional man. Where had he got his ideas *from*? What was his lineage? He had evidently been a figure of the kind that Hegel called 'world historical', a world moral hero whose significance transcended his immediate political circumstances and task; a man who belongs to all humanity. If there is anything at all in ethics and in the philosophy of life which is universal, such a man might be expected to embody it. So what is it?

We were not told. All we were given was a helpful reference to Gandhi as another figure of comparable stature, but no further details were forthcoming. Nobody asked. Along with natural philosophy, ethics is the oldest of all academic subjects, but it is not a subject to which people nowadays are ready to devote serious study and thought. The twentieth century was utterly consumed with vast ideological and national conflicts, huge worldwide population growth, and very rapid cultural and technical change. It was common by the later twentieth century to find that people at large had entirely forgotten the thought-world and leading ideas of the early twentieth century, so much had happened in the interim.

Nelson Mandela, like other African leaders of his generation, grew up after the First World War in the culture of Africa's Christian missionary schools. We might call that culture humanitarian now, but in those days it was simply Christian. Mandela could not fail to learn about the Bible and about the various British humanitarian movements, often led by Quakers and by Evangelical Christians, which had struggled since the Enlightenment for the emancipation of slaves and of many other groups, such as workers, women, prisoners, the insane and children. These social and political reformers had more or less invented Christian social ethics as a subject and had given it a good name; and in addition a new weapon had recently been forged for them. That is, in the mid-1870s Leo Tolstoy ran into a period of acute mid-life crisis and began to study the gospels intensively. Supernatural doctrine was out of the question for him, as it had been for George Eliot a little earlier, but like her he was strongly drawn to Christianity's last stronghold, variously described as 'the Sermon on the Mount' and 'the teaching of Jesus'. Tolstoy's study led him particularly to emphasize Jesus' call for thoroughgoing simplicity of life, nonviolence, and universal love and reconciliation; and Tolstoy developed these ideas in a string of books and tracts, many of them published in the 1880s and subsequently appearing in translation around the world. Tolstoy became himself a world moral hero, and his religious books had such a reputation that in Britain they were included in the Oxford University Press's *World's Classics* series.[2] A number of Tolstoyan communities were established, and the ideas of nonviolent protest and passive resistance remained prominent in public debate at least until the heyday of the Campaign for Nuclear Disarmament in the 1960s and 1970s. I read Tolstoy's religious writings in the Sixties, but they are not read now.

In India Tolstoy's influence was even stronger, especially through M. K. Gandhi, whose appropriation of the ethics of Jesus into the Hindu tradition influenced the Congress Party, especially in the Nehru years of 'non-alignment' during which India led a large group of peaceable nations who sought to keep clear of the great military confrontation between the capitalist West and the Communist East. In addition, Gandhi's early years of political activism in South Africa greatly influenced the emergent African National Congress (ANC)—and therefore the young Nelson Mandela. It is of course true that after the Sharpeville massacre the younger militants in the ANC could not be restrained, and there was some industrial sabotage, in which Mandela was involved. But the ANC did *not* embark upon the political assassinations and suicide bombings that have become so familiar to us nowadays, and from his later prison years onwards Mandela became even more a follower of the maxim: 'love your enemy'. In a continent whose politics is often a by-word for violence and corruption, he was extraordinarily equable, persistent, rational and magnanimous.

This very brief sketch is sufficient to remind us that Mandela did belong to a lineage that runs from Enlightenment humanism through such figures as Dickens, Tolstoy, Gandhi, Albert Schweitzer, Martin Luther King and then on to Mandela himself. Many other moral heroes might be added to the list: Byron, even Chaplin, and amongst the British humanitarians the early liberal John Locke, along with such figures as Coram, Clarkson, Elizabeth Fry, Hannah More, Wilberforce and Shaftesbury (the

Seventh Earl). If we were to continue expanding and extending the list, it would begin to include many popular entertainers of recent years: Seeger, Lennon, Dylan, Baez, Geldof. In addition, we could incorporate mention of a host of courageous 'aid workers'. But now we have enough, enough to make us think that even so unlikely a figure as the pope, by taking the name of Francis, hopes to be seen by us as admiring that same tradition. He'd like to be affiliated to it. He'd like us to see our modern activist humanitarian ethics as being through and through a product of the Christian tradition, and in particular as part of the legacy of Jesus and St Francis. He and the rest of them at the Vatican are well aware that after the collapse of neo-Thomism, Catholic Christianity is in acute intellectual trouble; but in its core moral values its appeal is as great as ever. Hence the striking fact that by putting doctrine on the back burner, and by foregrounding simple ethical gestures, Pope Francis has won world-wide praise—even from non-Christians.

We now have enough to see Mandela's ethics in historical perspective. Historic Christianity portrayed itself as having been born, not from the tradition of Jesus' ethical teaching, but as a supernatural hope. The faithful looked to heaven, awaiting the spectacular return of Jesus to establish his kingdom on earth. The believer was expected to be literally *vigilant,* and to spend much time in purifying himself so that he would be fit to meet the Lord. These early believers looked up to the supernatural world for their salvation: they were socially quietistic and religiously expectant. As for social ethics, it must wait till 'kingdom come'—an event that soon seemed to be receding further and further into the future. By the Middle Ages the original advent hope had been almost completely forgotten. The Church became 'indefectible' and its dogma 'immutable'; heaven itself was 'the Church triumphant', and the popes extended their own powers into the world of the dead by selling indulgences. Comparable ideas are also found among Protestants, who commonly held that during the present dispensation Jesus' ethic of nonviolent endlessly-forgiving love could be lived in private life, but because of human sinfulness could not prevail in the public sphere until the coming of the kingdom. Till then the state must rule by force. Thus the Protestant layman lived by an ethics of law and the legitimate use of coercive force in his official public life, but could and should become a Christian living by the ethics of the gospel when he shut his front door behind him at the end of the day and withdrew into the bosom of his family. In effect neither Catholics nor orthodox Protestants were expected to live out the teaching of Jesus in full. Not just yet. Not until after death, or 'kingdom come'. Hence it turned out that mainstream Christianity became essentially a private religion, whereas Islam still sees itself as essentially public.

Now look what happens. Classical Christianity developed almost no social ethics before the late nineteenth century: it developed only a penitential discipline and a 'moral theology' that was taught to priests in the seminaries and then applied to individuals in the confessional. The believer was chiefly concerned with self-purification. He needed to be 'in a state of grace', unsullied and ready; ready for worship, ready for the return of Christ, and ready for his own death. The whole system of thought and practice was in effect wholly and solely concerned with self-purification, worship and personal salvation after death. It was almost all worship and no ethics, in contrast with our more recent tradition of Quaker and Tolstoyan humanitarian activism, which can now be seen as a new secular version of Christianity that is all ethics and almost no worship. In this respect it has returned to the outlook of Jesus himself who, as biblical scholars are agreed, had no plans to found a new religion, and certainly not a religion based upon fanciful supernatural doctrines about himself and an even more fanciful cult of his own person.

The new activist Christianity follows the Quakers in protesting against the Church's long alliance with the civil power and its use of lethal force. It also largely discards church doctrine. Instead, it becomes determined to show that the ethical teaching of Jesus can be made to work here and now, in this present age. Like the Marxists, these new Christians see themselves as being here, not just to interpret the world but to change it. The old and deeply corrupt church-Christianity shrank away from worldly ethical struggle and commitment, and instead gave priority to the worship of the Most-Real (*ens realissimum*) and to supernatural doctrine. The new kingdom-Christianity rejects existing 'reality' and actively *posits* and builds a new moral world, Jesus' kingdom of nonviolent love. It plans *itself* to act out the long-promised passing away of the old world and the coming of a new world to replace it.

We thus open a very large question. Historically, our major religious traditions have contained two great themes or dimensions, namely worship, the systematically-ordered cult of the gods; and ethics, the government of human personal and social life in this world by religious values, or religious law.

In classical Christianity the single most influential text on the religious life was the *Rule of St Benedict*, composed at Monte Cassino in about 530 CE. It says in effect that the Christian ideal is to live a life that is overwhelmingly dominated by the Divine Office—basically, worship every three hours from now until the end of history—with only a token ethical supplement. In today's popular Christianity, the same idea is still current. Christianity is churchgoing, and that's all. We should keep our heads down, mind our own business, and keep out of politics. Politicians praise 'moderate' (which means privatized and otherworldly) religion. From Christians they still get a good deal of political acquiescence. But when they commend 'moderation' to Muslims they are on very shaky ground, because Muslims have *always* attempted comprehensively to Islamicize the public, social world. And, as we have seen, many Christians and activist post-Christians are nowadays tending to move in the same direction. For them Christianity is no longer an adoring celebration of what is presently Most Real, but an ethical decision to struggle patiently and lovingly to produce a new 'reality' in this life.

Now the big question which I need to address in this book at last comes into view. We are talking about a whole world-view—or rather, perhaps a whole view of life, in which instead of metaphysics (and in particular, ontology) coming first, ethical rejection of the world as we have received it comes first, with a decision to fill the resulting void with moral striving. We are talking about an ethics-led, rather than a metaphysics-led, way of life and vision of the world. In a post-philosophical and post-traditional culture such as ours now is, religion, philosophy and ethics—in short, *everything*, must eventually come out differently. We conquer today's moral dissatisfaction and pessimism—and even today's *nihilism*—by love, and not least by loving the utter transience in which we moderns are all of us immersed. We don't aim to *conserve* the self, preparing it for eternity: we simply *expend* it, by living generously. We are transient, and must *let go*.

What is all this like; or, what is it going to be like? During the past three hundred years faith in our received church Christianity has been growing more and more ironical, and our allegiance to it is now maintained for cultural reasons only. We love it for what it *used* to be: we love it for its legacy. Since the 1830s, or perhaps since Chateaubriand's *Génie du christianisme* (1802), Christianity in its European heartlands has been entirely replaced by a mood of yearning nostalgia for itself. We love that lost childhood world of neo-medieval architecture, of boy sopranos in surpliced choirs, of nativity plays and Christmas carols. Odd that as recently as Jane Austen's *Emma* (1816) Christmas can come and go without any of it—because it all expresses not Christianity, but nostalgia for a lost sacred cosmology. The great Christological dogmas of the divine Son's eternal genera-tion, co-equal divinity, incarnation, saving death, resurrection, ascension, heavenly session at the Father's right hand and so on come to us as reminders of a lost world-view; whereas the cluster of values that we associate with the teaching of Jesus (or perhaps rather, as some would say, with Luke, the third evangelist) have, in our modern world-moral-heroes, in much of our social practice, and in our great international aid organizations, become more authoritative and attractive than ever. Christos Pantocrator, Jesus as God's divine Son, dressed up like a Roman Emperor and sitting on a rainbow may still be a figure of some interest to art historians. Otherwise the Risen Lord is dead, whereas the dead Jesus lives: in the modern world, his ethic has largely conquered. His pioneering humanitarian ethics of love, and his dream of the possibility of a truly good society on earth only a step away, made possible the modern state's acceptance of moral responsibility for the education, the health and the welfare of all its citizens. Jesus' ethic permeates the whole service sector in modern Western economies, and especially all the institutions that care for the young, the elderly, the sick and others of the most vulnerable. We are not always successful: as I write we are failing to help Syrians as much as we should. But at least we do know that we ought to be doing something about their horrifying affliction.

Since *Jesus and Philosophy* (2009) I have argued that Jesus' critics were quite right to see his teaching as 'blasphemous' and as incipiently atheistic. Few facts about Jesus are as well-attested as the fact that many of his contemporaries, and especially many religious professionals, regarded him as a very bad troublemaker and heretic; and also the fact that the early church—presumably influenced by him—did indeed rapidly discard most of the old Jewish religious law, drawing a sharp distinction between religious law as a preparatory discipline, and the adult freedom of the gospel. The early Christians perhaps found it hard to appreciate what a big shift this was, for ethical monotheism was very strongly linked with the idea of the Creator as being first and foremost the cosmic Lawgiver. God's Word really was law.

In the beginning the Creator's commanding utterance had imposed his own regular order upon the primal chaos. In the more developed account, God imposed physical law upon the material world, the natural moral law upon finite spiritual substances (spirits and human souls), and also had given his revealed written law to his elect people. Against this background Jesus' distinctly free and easy attitude to the law was incipiently a revolt against God, as the great early theologian-heretic Marcion clearly saw.[3] And Matthew would not have made Jesus deny that he came to abolish the Law unless there were many people who were claiming exactly that about him.

By questioning whether a religion of strictly-applied divine law could ever create people who could live entirely without *ressentiment* (a French word borrowed by Nietzsche to signify ill-feeling of every kind) in a truly good society, Jesus started something—a tradition in which God abdicates by becoming human and dying, in man and for man. God, who in Christ has assumed generic humanity, then also pours himself out as living, highly-conscious Spirit into the whole human race. So Jesus started the ball rolling, and the Christian tradition has duly evolved into international (i.e., not ethnocentric) secular humanitarianism, today's dominant ethic. And it is not likely to be superseded. Jesus the dead teacher has done better than the divine Christ: he has converted almost the whole of humanity.

The one great exception to all this is Islam, which may be seen as the last and grandest attempt to create in public space the kingdom of God on earth *without* permitting any kind of humanist dissolution of God. God is *not* human, and does not become human. God remains God, and Islam—although it has accepted some influence of Jesus' teaching, for example by creating some philanthropic institutions such as the Red Crescent—has not wished to forget about life after death and become as intensely, emotionally, humanitarian and as much in love with this life's transient visual beauty as we others are.

Today we seem to be at a moment of decision. Looking at the world's main faith-traditions, ask yourself: Would I rather, along with Pope John-Paul II, turn away from Buddhism and turn first of all to the Muslim, because he like me believes above all else in the unity of God and in God's revealed will? Or, alternatively, would I rather (possibly along with Pope Francis, but who knows for sure?), would I rather turn first to the Buddhist, and discuss with him the similarities and differences between our mystical and our ethical traditions?

Which way you instinctively want to turn in the triangular debate between the three faiths has become a very urgent and important question. For my own part, my anti-realist philosophy and thoroughgoing humanism lead me to look towards Buddhism; but the history of Islam shows us a tradition that was formerly much broader and more varied than it sometimes appears today. We need to remain open to Islam, and to the possibility that Islam in diaspora in the West may soon have a lot more to say than we have yet heard from it.

I turn now to a different issue. Much of our discussion has turned upon the beliefs, firstly, that we can broadly describe the ethical teaching of the historical Jesus; secondly, that we can legitimately see modern Western humanitarian ethics as its lineal descendant; and, thirdly, that there is at least a broad analogy between the human condition as it presented itself to Jesus' first hearers and as we know it today. We need here to recall just how vehemently many modern theologians, and especially New Testament scholars, will reject all I have said.

For example, Albert Schweitzer argued that many nineteenth-century scholars had pursued 'the quest of the historical Jesus' in the belief that when they had found him he would serve as the basis for a reformation and renewal of Christianity. By the end of the nineteenth century, however, the most plausible reconstruction of Jesus's teaching was the theory of 'consistent eschatology' put forward by Johannes Weiss (1863–1914) in his book

The Preaching of Jesus about the Kingdom of God (1893). Jesus' whole task and message had been to proclaim the imminent and spectacular arrival of a supernatural kingdom of God, in which he himself would be manifested as the world-Messiah. Jesus had been found—but he was a figure whose highly counter-cultural world-view could never be taken seriously by modern people. Schweitzer endorsed Weiss's theory; but then went counter-cultural *himself* by leaving Europe and becoming a missionary doctor in Africa. So Schweitzer duly became himself a world moral hero, and a prominent modern follower of the very Jesus whom he had declared too strange to be followed by a modern person.[4]

A century later, there are two or three comments to be made upon Schweitzer's claim that Jesus' eschatological world-view is utterly strange to us. Even in Schweitzer's own day, not everyone was a long-term optimist about our human prospect: on the contrary, he knew all about Nietzsche's great pronouncement that 'Nihilism stands at the door',[5] an idea Nietzsche works out with terrifying thoroughness (and accuracy). Schweitzer also lived in a world in which Schopenhauer was highly influential, and Oswald Spengler would shortly publish *The Decline of the West* (1918–22). As for more recent years, I once tried to write down a full list of all the reasons why, between 'the atomic bomb' in 1945 and 'climate change' today, it has been widely feared amongst us that our world may soon be coming to an end. I gave up at fifteen. Far from being confined to Jesus' generation, talk of a catastrophic end of the world has long been part of our culture.

There is much more to add. Modern scientific naturalism has led, especially since late-Victorian times, to a general loss of belief in life after death. This has led millions of us into a very acute horror of death, coupled with an equally acute sense of our own utter transience and insignificance on a cosmic scale, and also to a number of eccentric attempts to cheat death by, for example, freezing severed heads until we have the technology to revive them.

Add also the fact that ordinary people who are having a very bad time are always apt to see life as the scene of a great war between the powers of good and evil, and it is clear that people in all ages, including ourselves, have found reasons for fearing that their life is profoundly threatened by its traditional uncertainties and limits—in short, Time, Chance and Death. To such people, Jesus' remedy is to say: '*Let go* of your fears and horrors, and worries; pour yourself out into your own transience, live like the sun, live by 'coming out', abandon all negative feeling, live expressively, live by the heart, live *out* emotively, live by love. You'll be living a dying life, passing away all the time along with everything else; and when you have identified yourself completely with the transience that so threatened you, you'll start to see it as mystically beautiful. This immanent mysticism of secondariness is profoundly consoling, and you'll find yourself living in a world that, like the heaven of the Bible, is all light, with nothing hidden or dark at all.'

Next we should briefly consider the objection that since Schweitzer's famous early book appeared there has been another century of intensive scholarly debate about the gospels, but it cannot report any gains. After source criticism, form criticism, redaction criticism, and even canon criticism, the common consensus is that the gospels as we have seen them are the product of several decades of intensive and fast-moving debate. There are so many layers of interpretation that they leave us with no prospect of ever finding a single face behind all the masks. For generations early Christianity was a running argument between many different schools of thought. It took centuries for a canonical 'orthodoxy' to evolve, and the more we study, the more we realize that the quest for a normative point-origin is vain.

That is true. It is also true that all ancient historians, biographers and storytellers freely invented the direct speech they put into the mouths of their characters. Accordingly, I do admit that the *person* of the historical Jesus is now forever inaccessible to us, and in any case I seek to avoid the cult of his person. All I need claim is that at the centre of the evolving tradition of his teaching there are unforgettably vivid themes and values that even church-Christians know all about. These sayings have created a moral tradition that endures to this day, and is admired around the world.

For many years I have felt that the Jesus of St John's Gospel and of much popular piety is an embarrassingly pallid, androgynous and unconvincing figure, and now I feel the time has come to rescue Jesus the moral teacher from what his own followers have made of him. It is not an easy task, because we cannot hope to hear more than very faint after-echoes of his original voice. In practice, we have only the history of the sayings-tradition to guide us, and I take the view that the Jesus of history remained strong in the tradition until the rise of the Easter faith and the conversion of Paul in the late 40s. Thereafter the supernatural Christ of Faith takes over, and the Jesus of history is quickly almost forgotten. But he needs to be heard again.

What Did
Jesus Teach?

At some point very early on in its development, Christianity split between two different pathways: one path stayed with the teaching of Jesus and the primacy of ethics, and the other path started with the return of Jesus and therefore with supernatural belief, holding that Jesus had been exalted to the heavenly world, whence he would in due course return in glory to establish his kingdom on earth. The main body of believers took this latter course, committing the faith to 'realistic' belief in God and in the supernatural world. On the practical side, the believers' main business was with worship and with self-purification so that one would in due course—probably after death—be ready to join him in the heavenly world.

Today supernatural belief, and metaphysics in general, are widely questioned. Belief in the old God is in unstoppable decline, even within the churches and amongst the clergy. Some form of language-mediated naturalism or neo-pragmatism is, philosophically speaking, the only game in town. In which case we must go back to the original parting of the ways, and explore what Christianity might look like today if it had stuck to the teaching of Jesus and the primacy of ethics. We can draw encouragement from the fact that the dominant modern ethical tradition of post-Enlightenment humanitarianism is clearly derived from and inspired by Jesus. We can replace faith and supernatural belief by a creative moral decision to become a kind of person, and to live a kind of life, that you might have thought to be beyond the average person's reach. So a kind of *ethical su-pernaturalism* that creates a new kind of self and a better society replaces the old *ontological supernaturalism* that even yet talks of 'another dimension' or 'a higher order of being'. What a relief to get rid of all that nonsense, and replace it with something that we can easily make true ourselves by deciding for it.

So far, so good. Now we need to state simply and clearly what the teaching of Jesus was, and how far we can appropriate it and live it today, in a different world and after all this time.

Suddenly, we meet a curious paradox. From the past we have inherited a number of purported summaries of Jesus' message; but they are unsatisfactory, because they fail to pick out the most distinctive features of his teaching.

From within the gospels themselves, we *first* pick out Mark 1:15: 'The time is fulfilled, and the kingdom of God is at hand; repent, and believe in the gospel.' I have paraphrased this saying at length elsewhere:[6] it was standard teaching amongst the rabbis that if Israel fully observed the law for one day, the Kingdom would come. Which implies that the law is already sufficient to win our salvation, and does not lead us to expect any significant *additional* moral teaching from Jesus. The final clause, 'repent, and believe' sounds like the language of the Church, and not the language of Jesus, who was not a dogmatic teacher.

Secondly, there is the well-known 'Lord's Summary of the Law' (Mark 12:28–34 and parallels), which invokes Deuteronomy 6:4 and Leviticus 19:18, and is merely a stock answer that quotes accepted scripture. People often quote the Leviticus line, 'love thy neighbour as thyself', as if it were in itself a satisfactory summary of Jesus' teaching. But elsewhere Jesus himself is sharply critical of mere reciprocity as sufficient in ethics.

Thirdly, the same retort must be made in the case of 'the Golden Rule', 'do as you would be done by'. This maxim crops up in many ancient schools of wisdom, and is not by any means uniquely from Jesus.

Fourthly, there is the Lord's Prayer, often taught in catechisms as a kind of summary of Jesus' religion. Again, it is evidently a church composition which does not close, but rather *reaffirms* the very distinction—indeed the separation—between the heavenly and earthly worlds, that Jesus sought to *close*.

And, *fifthly*, some people may cite the best-loved of all the parables—that is, the parables of the Good Samaritan and the Prodigal Son—as epitomizing the ethics of Jesus, with the presumed lessons that God will always forgive, and that one should help the needy. But both of these parables have reached us in a written form that is wholly St Luke's. You may retort that the moral of each story is surely in Jesus' own spirit; but the lesson in each case is not quite what you may think. The Good Samaritan story is anti-racist, and the second story brings out very forcefully the Elder Brother's ressentiment, his sheer meanness of spirit.

The failure of all these standard attempts to summarize Jesus' message is highly instructive. Over and over again, in the best received traditions, Jesus is very sharply critical of ordinary people's lust for crushingly-violent retribution. 'I want *closure*, and I cannot get it except by purging all of my accumulated ill-feeling'. And he is equally sharply critical of any morality of balanced reciprocal rights and duties within the brotherhood created by an accepted body of religious law. You haven't *begun* to understand Jesus until you have burst out of that framework of easy mutual backscratching.

When in 1985 the Fellows of the Jesus Seminar of Santa Rosa, California, embarked upon a systematic and public search for the original teaching of Jesus, they began by listing 1330 units of tradition—sayings and stories that have come down to us in the Gospels of Matthew, Mark, Luke, John and Thomas. They defined their criteria of historicity (or 'authenticity') carefully, and then discussed and voted upon all the sayings.[7] Only twenty-nine sayings made the top grade—sayings in which we seem to hear something close to Jesus' own voice. Most of these top-grade sayings were found in Q, the sayings-gospel or collection of Jesus' sayings that was drawn upon by both Matthew and Luke. Amongst the sayings that attracted most votes of all were a few very-familiar ones commending extreme magnanimity and generosity. These most-favoured sayings were Q/Matthew 5:39 ('turn the other cheek'), Q/Matthew 5:40 ('when sued for your cloak, give your coat too'), Q/Luke 6:20 ('blessed are the poor'), Q/Matthew 5:41 ('go the second mile'), and Q/Luke 6:27 ('love your enemies').

On the view that I have proposed, we know little of the historical Jesus, and certainly not enough to justify any cult of his person. Nor do we have any of his *ipsissima verba* (his very own words). But the traditional body of moral teaching that springs from him does seem to have at its core the idea that we shall not become fully good and happy members of a fully-reconciled society unless we learn to be 'big'—capable of reaching out to the other, capable of making the first move, and capable of taking the risk of being consistently generous and forgiving even to those who have wronged us most badly. Above all, we must never nurse ill feeling or harbour a grudge, because that kind of negative feeling, ressentiment, feeds upon itself and poisons the soul.

St Paul turned Jesus' teaching into Christianity, and in doing so badly damaged it, by putting first not a spontaneous outflow from the individual human heart, but his claim that *God* has acted first, reaching out to us in Christ in an act of unmerited generosity that saves us from our sins and 'reconciles the world to himself'. Our part is simply to respond to God's gracious initiative. In this way St Paul attempts to take the stinging radicalism out of Jesus' teaching and restore the priority of the old gracious patriarchal order at cosmic level. In the old prophets, God was already seen as lovingly and patiently trying to win faithless Israel back to himself. (See, for example, Hosea 2:14–20.) But in such cases the mutual love between God and Israel is enfolded within a covenant that makes loyalty to it morally *obligatory*, a matter of pre-established religious *duty*. Jesus follows the prophets in saying that this old religion of sacred law has proved unable to make people consistently virtuous. Interestingly, the reason for this is partly logical: laws may prohibit classes of action, but there will always be marginal cases, and no code of law can cover absolutely everything and reach into all corners of the human heart, just as no system of taxation can collect quite 100 percent of the taxes due. There will always be scope for tax avoidance and tax evasion. In that latter case, we'd do better to look for ways of making people fully public-spirited and generous, so that they pay their taxes in full, and do so voluntarily because it is in their own interest to do so. Somewhat similarly, Jeremiah (see 31:31–34) and Jesus say that human beings and human society won't become what they should be until we have a new ethics of the heart. In modern philosophical terms, Jesus' outlook is emotive and expressivist. He seems to see life, or as we might call it 'libido', as welling up in 'the heart' and flowing out into expression in our symbolic words and behaviours in the common social world. When the flow of feeling is free-running and free from any ressentiment, we will naturally be completely open, transparent and loving in our dealings with each other. There will be no 'discrimination' and no darkness: everything will be as clear as daylight. Jesus' outlook appears to be naturalistic: there is, at least in the core sayings, only one world, and it is *this* world. Both Israel and the Church were bounded societies, with a clear line between the brotherhood and the 'heathen' outsiders, who may well be powerful and hostile; but Jesus envisages a 'Kingdom' world and a Kingdom-ethic which does *not* discriminate, and tries instead to be as widely and generously inclusive as possible. He seems to be calling for a limitlessly self-forgetting love, beyond what people in the past had thought possible—and perhaps even beyond *God*. The Kingdom does not have its own internal structure, and does not defend itself. It is an invisible society of the Spirit, not a visible institution.

All of this may seem strange, but the ideal is still familiar, and still persuasive. Nelson Mandela, as South African President, took the risk and demonstrated the point when he dressed up as a fan to cheer the (all White) South African national rugby football team. He wanted to show people that he really was committed to a post-racist society, a rainbow nation. And on the intellectual side, the liberal socialist philosopher Jürgen Habermas is clearly still drawing upon Jesus and the Kingdom-tradition when he describes an 'ideal speech-situation' as a model to guide thinking about the ethics of a future socialist world in which there is no longer any kind of domination or duplicity, and people have become completely open to each other.

Before the argument resumes, one large and difficult question needs to be mentioned. It is well known that Jesus seems not to have taught, nor even much concerned himself with, the ethics of sex. But by using the word *libido* above I prompted the reader to wonder whether his kingdom world must inevitably become a world of Free Love. In the past people have often been irked by the Church's many ambiguous and unsuccessful attempts to police human sexuality, and they have dreamt of—indeed, they have tried to establish—small perfectionist communities of 'Free Love', with decidedly mixed results.

I raise, but cannot discuss this point further here. In our own culture, thinking about sexual politics and about the future social management of human sexualities is in flux, and none of us can guess where the argument may be in a few generations' time.

Meanwhile, the present situation could scarcely be worse. For historical reasons the Church's teaching on sexual matters is a mess, and its own practice is too often shockingly corrupt; and as for a 'Kingdom' sexual ethic, we don't yet know what sort of shape it should have.

I have been trying to argue that by far the best of what's left of Christianity is the great tradition of patient nonviolent struggle for large-scale humanitarian social reform since the Enlightenment, which looks back ultimately to the Sermon on the Mount.[8] Why can't we persuade people to move from a worship-first to an ethics-first vision of Christianity, seeing Jesus not as a cosmic king, but simply as the human moral teacher that he was? The so-called "Death of God" and the end of metaphysics are today seen by many people as presenting us with a crisis of nihilism, but I hope to show that an ethics-led interpretation of faith can inspire us to get out of nihilism by choosing a new sort of selfhood in a new human world. Unfortunately, the contemporary churches are in such a deplorable moral and intellectual state that they have dissipated all the high public esteem that Christian ethics slowly built up during the period since the French Revolution. We are left with an uphill struggle.

How are we to pursue that struggle? In the traditional theocentric and worship-led version of Christianity, the way to sainthood was by giving top priority to self-purification and one's personal attainment of eternal salvation. One sought to make oneself fit for God's presence.

The ethics-led version of Christianity takes a very different view. The struggle to live the Dream in advance demands expressive, extravertive, solar and self-forgetful living without any ressentiment. Sainthood is not for its own sake: the self is simply expended. But we must strive for saintliness if we want to bring into being a better world for other and future people.

Scattered
and Gathered

In Britain especially, for the past century or so it has been common to speak of God as being 'both transcendent and immanent'. The formula is not traditional, and I think it may have been given currency by a Victorian theologian, J. R. Illingworth, who used it to differentiate orthodoxy from the thoroughgoing immanentism of the German Idealists that was then becoming pervasive.[9] In those days it became a joke that a well-known Modernist, asked if he still believed in the divinity of Christ, replied: 'Far be it from me to deny *anyone's* divinity.'

All that sort of thing is out of date now, and we should discard the 'both transcendent and immanent' formula, and replace it with a much older and better one, to the effect that God, the sacred generally, the people of God, and the individual self may be thought of as being in one or the other of two contrasting phases or states: they may be gathered, focussed, concentrated, recollected, assembled, unified and 'returned'; or they may be scattered over the hills and across the whole field of experience, dispersed, disseminated, outpoured, emigrated, outgoing, discomposed or exiled.

This great contrast is very prominent in the 'metaphoric' of both the Jewish and the Christian scriptures. In a straightforward and popular sense, much of human life has for millennia been seen as following a rhythm of going out to 'the field' in the morning and returning into one's home each evening; or gathering weekly in God's more focussed presence at one's local place of assembly for worship, and then scattering to go about one's daily business during the week. In society, the human self is relatively dispersed into its own role-playing. It is extraverted, turned outwards; but in solitude the self becomes more introvertive and recollects itself, gathers itself together and becomes more conscious of itself before God (*coram Deo*).

The case of God is particularly important and instructive. The most-highly 'concentrated' forms in which God appears in the Bible—the burning bush, the summit of Mount Horeb/Sinai, the Ark, and one or two Temple-visions—are found only in the Old Testament, are commonly set in the remote, mythic past, and can be lethal.[10] Only Moses is holy enough to be able to take the full blast of God's 'presence'.

God is less fiercely concentrated and dangerous when he appears at one remove. As a king may be represented by an ambassador, so God may appear in the form of an angel, or even in more-or-less human form as a great king. Thus lightly veiled, divinity becomes easier to speak with.

Now note: in the New Testament, and in Christianity generally, God *never* appears in his most concentrated and terrifying form. Occasionally he appears in the form of a human Voice in the sky, but otherwise he typically appears in the human form of Jesus Christ the King—for example, in *Revelation*, in much of Byzantine art, and in Jan Van Eyck's Ghent altarpiece. In more veiled forms, God may be 'sensed' at the symbolic focus of the Church, hovering just above the altar or the icon-screen, or perhaps embodied in the human person (the Holy Father) positioned at the summit of the organized, visible and patriarchal church-institution. Then God is further dispersed, first into mankind at large, and then into the sublime in Nature. At last, in the *Tenebrae* ritual after the death of Jesus on Good Friday,

God is finally dispersed into the darkness and objectivity of his own death. A rather similar progressive dispersal of God into humanity, into nature and finally into his own death takes place in other faith-traditions too. Certainly Christian iconography as it develops consistently shows the tradition of faith developing into the death of God and the triumph of an approximately Wordsworthian world-mysticism combined with humanitarian ethics.

The story that I have briefly recalled points to two different, and indeed, *opposite* ways in religious thought. As I have argued elsewhere, the early Jesus was a thoroughgoing scatterer: his teaching-tradition preserves a memory of his argument as having been emotivist, expressivist, outgoing, heedless, very short-termist, imprudent, carefree and self-expending. He rushes towards his fate because he has no time for ressentiment, nor for any thoughts of escape. Generous to the point of supererogation, he is always reck-less. Very interestingly, his core teachings *always* exhibit three main themes: rejection as self-poisoning of the ordinary person's vindictive demand for justice, 'closure', 'a level playing-field' and so on; rejection of every single form of ressentiment in favour of complete availability and openness towards others; and insistence that one must be always and unhesitatingly *over*-generous in one's response, always going beyond what custom and law require. Make a point of overdoing it. Give the *Big Issue* seller two pounds, and not one.

So much for the movement in religious life and thought that sees the self as always living in the Now-moment, and always pouring itself out into the public world and social expression. This fits well into our modern cosmology that sees the whole universe as an explosive out-pouring and passing away, 'the Fountain'. It makes Man the Microcosm, as the best religion and philosophy always did. But Matthew in particular gives prominence to a later, post-50s, Jesus who is becoming a sort of *Ur*-Catholic. Turning away from the transient and unsatisfactory external world, he seeks eternal happiness through introversion, recollection, inwardness, subjectivity. A long-termist, he is busy purifying himself and laying up treasure in heaven. He is prudent, not reckless. He is in every sense *careful* and *mindful*. He is an amphibian, someone who consciously lives with one eye on the transient world in which, for the present, he still lives, and another eye on the eternal world which is his true home. He lives a relatively ascetic life now, for the sake of eternal happiness in the next world. He believes not in immediacy but in deferred satisfactions.

For the original Jesus, the kingdom of God has already come as soon as we begin to live its life, finding eternal happiness in 'solar' living *now*, with heedless generosity; whereas for the later 'protocatholic' Jesus we live within the Church and accept its disciplines in the hope that the Church will deliver us into eternal happiness hereafter. The original Jesus says, 'Do it now! Don't look back! Don't calculate the costs and the benefits!' The later Jesus says, 'Prepare yourself, purify your hearts, put worship first, look to the eternal world, and to the things that are of eternal value!'

Briefly, the original Jesus was well remembered for up to two decades after his death, and some of his characteristic sayings were preserved long enough to get into Q. But from about the year 50 and the arrival of Paul, the original Jesus began to be transformed into the Catholic Jesus, mainly because supernatural belief was returning with such force. Jesus himself had been concerned to persuade people to live the unity of the two worlds in the Now-moment of ethical decision. He didn't look forward to a supernatural world *hereafter*; his 'supernatural' ethic gave him the supernatural world *now*, and in his own present activity. But later, the Church, as it came to believe in Jesus' assumption into heaven, and even his bodily resurrection and imminent return to earth in glory, reinstated long-termist and heaven-oriented spirituality. Fortunately St Luke, and even St Paul himself, successfully preserved a little of the spirituality of the original Jesus, so that when during the Second Millennium the faith of the friars began to turn towards this world, it could seize upon the fragments of the original Jesus that survive in the gospels, and from them develop a new Christian humanitarianism which nowadays is robust and appealing enough to entrench itself and survive around the world in secular form. Perhaps people are judging that we no longer need the original Jesus. His ethic and his spirituality can be relied upon to survive without his support after he is forgotten.

Maybe: we shall see. For the present I have a very striking conclusion to draw from our present discussion of God as intensely concentrated burning holiness and God scattered as the sublime in Nature, or as 'the candle of the Lord', the still small voice within each human being's inner emptiness and silence. The distinction is very interesting, but it is religious poetry, and not yet philosophical monotheism. The later God of the philosophers may now be seen as an attempted synthesis of the two visions: at every point in space and time the whole godhead is present 'by essence, presence and power', as Aquinas puts it. Another saying describes God as 'an infinite circle whose centre is everywhere and whose circumference is nowhere.' This is no doubt designed to exclude henotheism, the doctrine that we are exclusively loyal to one (finite) god whom we call Yahweh or 'the Lord', whereas other peoples serve other gods—a common Old Testament doctrine. Full philosophical monotheism has grasped the idea of God's infinity, and wants to proclaim his absolute and exclusive unity, and does so by cramming his entire white-hot godhead into every point in time and space, so that where God is God, then there cannot possibly be any other God, and finite, created souls and spirits cannot possibly have any other central concern of their existence except the worship of God just for being God. Hence Christian Platonism; hence the monks and their contemplative life, the *bios theoretikos*.

Against this background, could Jesus be described as an all-out philosophical monotheist, as Muslims perhaps still can? I guess not. Jesus' God, if any, is very 'scattered'. Jesus is primarily sociable, rather than mystical. He teaches an ethic of human relationships, rather than an exclusive, theocentric, fiery spirituality of the fully developed catholic type. And I guess that most readers of these words, if they grasp what it may mean to hold that the whole white-hot fury of the godhead is omnipresent in space and time, will conclude that such an overwhelming notion of God is badly overloaded. It makes the contemplative life of a monk or nun not just the best life, but almost the only imaginable life for a rational human being. It was bound to start crumbling as, at the end of the Middle Ages, human beings began to turn their attention to secular life, secular knowledge and human love.[11]

I hope we are now seeing that ideal of life coming to an end. With it, we need to see the end of religious celibacy, and of life under rule. As for Jesus, his God was at the least very scattered, and he himself is scattered to the four winds in death. He taught an ethic of self-scattering love—not love that clings, but love that *lets go*.

In so saying, I reject outright the liberal theology that is usually said to begin with F. D. E. Schleiermacher (1768–1834). Schleiermacher tried to preserve something of the older mediaeval religion by attributing to Jesus an unusually vivid personal experience of God and sense of dependence upon God. Liberal theology connected this with Jesus and with us by citing his alleged use of the word *abba* (Mark 14:36), which is quoted by St Paul. This 'simple faith' that calls God 'Father', or even 'Daddy', has been widely commended during the past two centuries as an adequate modern replacement for encountering the God of Moses, or for enjoying the Vision of God that was pursued by the contemplative monks! So appallingly infantile has much modern piety become.

The Glory
and the Dream

The notion of raw, violent unmediated divinity is so fascinating that we need to stay a little longer with it, briefly tracing the ways in which it slips away and disperses itself, and what happens next after it finally disappears.

An analogy for raw divinity and the demands it imposes: the very first angry yell of your own new-born baby, a moment in human life that I have compared with the Big Bang because of the sudden overwhelming violence of the presence it announces and the demand it makes. You smile; you are very pleased—and you know that this furious, purple little creature is now securely tied to you for the remainder of your life.

There are some good observations on the confrontation with raw divinity in Exodus 33, the chapter about the Tent of Meeting. The metaphors are drawn from friendship, face-to-face confrontation with full eye contact, and (as usual) a consuming fire.

Israel is about to march into the Promised Land. God will send an angel with the vanguard, but will not 'go up among you' in person, 'lest I consume you in the way, for you are a stiff-necked people.' For his own encounters with God, Moses establishes a special tent outside the main encampment. There 'the Lord used to speak to Moses face to face, as a man speaks to his friend.' Moses asks for more continuous full presence and support from God, to help him bear the burden of leadership. God in effect replies, 'Not even you could bear to remain permanently in my full face-to-face presence. No man can see God and live.' Still Moses persists: 'Show me thy glory'. To end this bargaining, God concedes a partial revelation: '. . . while my glory passes by I will put you in a cleft of the rock, and I will cover you with my hand until I have passed by; then I will take away my hand, and you shall see my back; but my face shall not be seen' (Exodus 33, RSV).

Although he is regarded in the Hebrew Bible as the greatest of human beings, not even Moses can bear the sight of raw, unmediated divinity for long. So God has to veil himself a little, even for his own chief witness and spokesman. The images are familiar. The Vision of God is overwhelming, like direct eye contact with a great king, or like trying to gaze directly at the sun. But if so, how was it that pure philosophical monotheism, by making God's own self ubiquitous in all space and time, has us spending our entire lives in a twenty-million-degree nuclear furnace from which we are presently shielded, and then promises us that the goal of human life, for every single one of us, is that we shall have the privilege of spending all eternity gazing head-on and immediately into that blinding, lethal white heat? One wonders how far a highly gifted early Modern man like Calvin knew what he sought and what he was promising to others. And it is not surprising that much of the history of religion, since antiquity, has been a history of God's merciful and progressive self-veiling in human flesh and in secondariness (that is, his appearance is not direct but mediated by something else), until at last he dies altogether, leaving only a mysticism of light and of human eye-contact, *Ich und Du*, You and I, which survived as the only metaphors that can help us to understand what it was all supposed to be about.

It needs to be mentioned here that there have been, and still are, attempts to revive and to explain the full sense of the

Sacred. The best is Islam's attempt fully to democratize daily contact with God's own godhead. Each individual member of the *umma*, saying the daily prayers, relates himself immediately to God. As I understand the traditional metaphoric, God is as near to us as our own jugular vein, or our own breathing. He is within, unseen because he is on the *near* side of the visual field. Our own physical humanity acts as the veil: there is a certain analogy between the praying Muslim's relation to God and the orthodox definition of the relation of the two Natures in Jesus Christ. In which case Islam may indeed be sort of true, because it has a more developed and democratized account of the divine-human relationship than Christianity has. But I think this question is too sensitive, and therefore has never been openly and courageously discussed. Perhaps nobody dares discuss it? Perhaps nobody wishes to?

The other interesting modern attempt to revive and democratize the ancient sense of the Sacred, in order to give modern humans a way back to a primal and authentic sense of God, is of course that presented by Rudolf Otto in his book *The Idea of the Holy* (1917). Unlike William James, Otto argued that there is such a thing as a distinctively religious feeling. He appealed not only to the typical encounters of Moses with God in the Jewish Torah, but also to a wide range of experiences of 'the numinous' in classical literature, where spirits are associated with particular sacred sites such as caves, streams and groves. Suddenly one remembers that the Hebrew Bible's encounters of a select human being with God take place at specific sites, which are named. Such holy places, where you go on pilgrimage to seek out and address a particular holy person, are absent from Protestantism but are still familiar to Catholics. In a particular place of appearance and of revelation, you can find privileged access to the sacred being, or the Saint, whom you need to approach.

To us, the illuminating realization is that just as much as the oracle at Delphi, the God of biblical monotheism began as a *genius loci*, a spirit tied to a particular holy place to which you must go to find him or her. The spirit is not found *except* at the established place of revelation. In which case the ancient Platonists who took Moses' experience of the most-intensely raw-and-pure Sacred at Mount Horeb/Sinai and elsewhere, and tried to *universalize* it across all space and time were making a false move. They make a logical mistake, and they badly *over-loaded* their idea of God.

Wittgenstein stated the vital counter-argument very clearly. When we judge that someone is mad, we are contrasting his condition with a background normality in which we can ordinarily assume everyone's sanity. When we judge that a coin is forged, we contrast it with a normal background state of things in which everyone feels safe in assuming that coins are authentic. And when we say that at Mount Sinai Moses encountered the Sacred in a uniquely intense and fearsome way—*mysterium tremendum et fascinans*—as Yahweh the God of Israel, we are contrasting Moses' awesome vision with a background of ordinary *secular* experience in which God is not present at full strength. In none of these cases is it rational to generalize the (definitionally) exceptional, and claim that it is the rule everywhere. It would not make sense to claim that '*every one* of us is mad, really', or that '*all* coins are forged', or that the terrifying, lethal, unapproachable holiness of the God who appeared to Moses at Sinai is ubiquitous in space and time. It shouldn't have been suggested that everywhere and always God is just like *that* for us. But once the error had become canonized within the main tradition of Western theism it became hard to shift, despite the strange paradoxes and incongruities that it generated.

Consider how, in the *Rule of Saint Benedict*, choir monks are told not to hang around at the monastery gate, gossiping with casual passers-by. 'You are not to enjoy talking to a fellow human being. You are a member of a small contemplative élite. Get back to your cell!' And consider again how the teaching of Jesus totally *lacks* the old Mosaic sense of the awesome holiness of God. He would have been amongst the gossips at the gate. He was just a sociable human being. His religion is concerned with the common human world, and with that only.

I have been suggesting that high philosophical monotheism was from the first an intellectual error, and that it generated a kind of antihuman, celibate, solitary religion suitable only for a very small class of hermit-intellectuals. But from the beginning it was evident that God must veil himself, or be veiled, if human beings were not to be ruined by him. As it turned out, the more recent veiling and scattering of God has taken place over the centuries along three different pathways. All three of them involve bringing God down into the process of things in this world.

First, God might fade down into Society, and symbolize the greatness of its power and the demands it makes of us. Often there is a pyramid of father-figures over the individual's head. In Moscow, the Third Rome, God was the Great Father hidden in the heavens above, the tsar was the more visible Little Father, and then came the ecclesiastical hierarchy of the Patriarch, your own diocesan Father in God, and your local spiritual father, the parish priest. In both the Eastern and the Latin Churches there was a strong tendency 'to fetishize the apparatus of mediation'. The big and complex machinery that was supposed to link you *to* God became *itself* in effect the religious object. This happens particularly in the case of those aesthetic cultural Christians who love all things 'churchy'. They have replaced true religion with churchiness.

Secondly, God fades down into the visual 'glory' of the passing stream of phenomena. We have become much more aware of this since in the mid-nineteenth century the new chemical engineering began to use aniline dyes and make a far wider range of colours than ever before available to artists. A string of very gifted painters began to create what I can only call a religion of visual experience. Their work occasionally produces in us a kind

of rapturous explosion. This has happened to me with Edouard
Manet occasionally, Claude Monet often, in Camille Pissarro's
late work, Seurat's and Signac's outdoor *pointilliste* scenes,
Kandinsky going into abstraction, Vincent van Gogh irregularly,
and (perhaps surprisingly) the later Bridget Riley. These artists,
and a few others too, have done much to give back to us and restore in us 'the glory and the dream' that Wordsworth knew that
he had lost, and thought he could never regain. This visual glory
is like Seeing God—God scattered into the glittering stream of
phenomena and the radiance of colours. It is so strong that it can
and does help to awake in us an unquenchable love of the world,
and of the whole transient stream of things, that since the death
of the old God has become the consolation of our life. We are
ourselves a part of the streaming visual bliss we contemplate. It is
infused with, and partly shaped by, our language and our feeling.
So we are happy to go *with* it all.

Thirdly, since the mid-nineteenth century we have come to
value more and more highly just the going-on of things in the
world of everyday life. The first person to use the formula 'Life is
God' was, so far as I know, Leo Tolstoy; but it should be noted
here that in your culture and mine it is women who, more than
men, have traditionally relished all the banal details of everyday
life—a capacity I now admire.

From this you will gather that the slow dispersal of God over
the past few centuries has brought the heavenly and earthly
worlds together, and has greatly enriched our common experience. We are immersed in transient bliss, easygoing—happy to
be passing. That is one half of the religion available to us now.
The other half that I have to add and also to defend is ethical.
It has to do with the ethical decision by which I conquer dread
and commit myself to my own transient part in the general human condition, and to solar living. I have to explain in detail
why I need the strangely excessive ethics of Jesus to keep ressentiment at bay and say an unqualified Yes to life. That excess

creates an exhilarating freedom and a space in which one can enjoy eternal happiness, for now. So I am talking about a second Christianity—the kingdom religion that we might have had now, if Jesus' whole vision had actually come to pass the first time round. As things have turned out, the full realization of his eschatology—his message about the coming of the last world, and about how we should live in it—has only finally come about in modern times.[12]

Creation, Divine
and Human

Before the arrival of the new ways of thinking associated with the romantic movement in the late
eighteenth century, it was rare for anyone to think
or even suggest that human beings can be truly creative. A partial exception was the bringing-forth, or production, of a baby,
which could be described as *procreation*; but otherwise the only
impressive human creator was a king, who by a simple act of his
will could bring into being a new law, a new title or a new institution. In the King's writing-room a document was prepared
announcing the new creation, and the King then made it official
by signing it and causing his Seal to be affixed to it. Thereafter,
one copy remained lodged in a record office for reference. But
it is not *itself* the new-created thing: it is rather the official record of an act of the king's sovereign will, by which a new rule,
complex of rules, or rule-governed entity, has been established
within the king's realm. Remember also that there will need to
be some form of official proclamation or promulgation to ensure
that those who will be bound by the new law do indeed get to
hear about it.

So much for the only important *secular* use of the verb 'to
create' that existed before the Enlightenment. The king's word
created and maintained the social order. Where his writ ran, his

word was law. It was published in various ways, and it was your duty to know it.

Two more steps in the argument. First, before the great explosion of human knowledge that began soon after the Reformation, the State was the largest and most complex law-abiding, 'organic' and enduring totality known; its only important rival being the human body. Throughout the Bible, for example, the Universe is pictured as a cosmic version of the State. It may be governed by a mountain-dwelling committee of gods, under the Presidency of a great sky-father; or, in the monotheistic versions, the Universe is politically an absolute monarchy. In the heavenly court, God is served by a large host of ministers who do his bidding. Either way, the top God is the great lawgiver. Being rational God is himself law-abiding, at least in the sense of being constant, reliable and true to himself. 'The being of God is a kind of law to his working', as Richard Hooker put it; and from God descended an enormously complex hierarchy of different kinds of law, applying to angels and to men, to natural agents and to rational, moral agents. It included both laws that were already built into the way the cosmos ran every day, and a written law specially revealed by God in order to open to sinful men a path to everlasting salvation.

In short, the whole of Creation had come into being as the will of God had imposed a vast, complex system of law and order upon the primal chaos.[13]

I say all this by way of recalling the enormous, cosmic significance of the idea of divine law in prescientific culture. Christians tend to forget this point, partly because they have now become familiar with the mathematical-mechanistic view of the world associated with natural science, and partly because a large part of the old Jewish law (even if, technically, it was only 'the ceremonial law') was abrogated by the early church in apostolic times, and partly because what is *now* the standard Christian doctrine of *creatio ex nihilo* tells a rather different story. The new doctrine was defined at the Fourth Lateran Council in 1215. Against a background of threatening dualist heresy, newly influential Aristotelian and other Greek ideas about ontology and about the eternity of matter, and disputes about sovereignty, the new doctrine strongly stressed the total and continuing dependence of every finite thing upon the creative will of God. In effect the new doctrine shifted the main emphasis somewhat from law to being, and has thereby hidden from us the older vision of a cosmos pervaded from top to bottom by divine law. In brief, religious law was as pervasive in the monotheistic cultures as was dharma in Buddhism and the Dao in China. And to this day Judaism and Islam remain religions of divine law to a much greater degree than Christianity.

Only when we understand all this can we grasp why Jesus' notorious laxity about religious law caused such intense opposition and hostility on the part of his critics. It could easily have seemed to them to be incipiently atheistic. It threatened faith in a whole sacred construction of the world, and in its Creator.

Even today, the point is still very sensitive. It shows up, for example, in the very different ways in which Jews and Christians read the Hebrew Bible. For the Jews, the Mosaic Law *is* the Bible, to such a degree that many people are not very familiar with the Prophets and the Writings. Christians, on the other hand, studied the Prophetic books very closely in early times in order to pick out passages that seemed to them prophetic of Jesus, and also passages that described the nation's historic failure to keep the law satisfactorily, and the need therefore for a new and perhaps even *supralegal* way to salvation—salvation, not by obeying the law, but by accepting an unmerited divine forgiveness.

Now in ancient times it was generally thought that to be happy we need to be able to see the world as a readymade and stable divine order, a 'creation' governed by a benevolent absolute Monarch. It was, of course, a highly non-historical view of

the world, and a 'box' that nobody yet knew how to think outside. Some writings do survive which show us just how traumatic
it was for an ancient human to live through the breakdown, by
military defeat and acute political instability, of the blessed divine
physical *and moral* order of things to which he or she had always
been accustomed. The world crashes: the gods die—and life is
'meaningless'.

By general consent, Jesus was at least in some degree, and
even perhaps predominantly, an eschatological prophet. He
announced the end, or at least the imminent end, of an entire
vision of the world and régime of religious law. The individual
was going to be suddenly deprived of everything that supported
him and told him how he should live. This was like a return into
the primal chaos, as described in Genesis 1:2a: 'The earth was
without form and void and darkness was upon the face of the
deep . . .' (RSV). The beloved old order was passing away and
could no longer give us any guidance. It needed to be washed
away, and the individual, *exactly* like God in the Genesis story,
needed actively to use language to set out, to affirm, and to enter into a new construction of the world, a new understanding
of the self, and new values. You would be like a child who takes
a piece of chalk and marks out the playing-area for a new game
to play. *You* have to set up a world for *yourself* to play in, as that
little girl does.

Thus the celebrated Genesis creation-narrative, or narratives,
may on the surface seem to describe in the language of myth
how the Creator first established the old sacred divine order; but
beneath that surface the story is telling us how after the death
of the old Creator and his great régime of cosmic order, we can
find the courage and the strength to lay down, and to choose a
new life in, a long-promised new world.

Look at how in the biblical story God himself begins by being in darkness. His gradually-emergent consciousness drifts
and dozes above the dark waters. He chooses light and abruptly

awakens, empowered for world-building. That's a message for *you*. Wake up, choose life! Now you have a world before you, in which you can do your own thing, act your part and fulfill your purposes. Thus human beings are called to create their way out of nihilism, very much as God did 'in the beginning'. As I've said at length elsewhere, the idea of God is a 'leading' idea: it functions as a role model for us.

Against this background we can guess how extremely radical the early message of the Galilean Jesus was, and how sharply it divided his hearers. He seemed to be announcing the imminent end of a great epoch or 'dispensation' of sacred history. The old, comfortable gap between the heavenly and earthly worlds was closing, and its closure would make all the equally old and familiar channels of communication between the two worlds redundant. A whole sacred construction of reality that had been established for centuries was now coming to an end. The new revelation would make the old one 'history'.

To some of Jesus' hearers, this must have seemed a very dark and threatening message. He appeared to think he had come 'to abolish the law and the prophets', and even to announce the destruction of the Temple. The message was at least incipiently blasphemous and even atheistic because it seemed to announce the destruction of all existing moral reality, and to make Jesus' new ethic a form of pure emotivism.

But to others of Jesus' hearers the message was a liberating 'gospel', good news. For them, the old order was not so comfortable. On the contrary, it was religiously and also often *morally* oppressive. God was at the summit of a great cosmic hierarchy of mediators: the eternal Torah, the angels, and on earth the armies of priests and of men who copied the text of the law, expounded and interpreted it, and applied it in the religious courts. The divine was very remote; whereas in the new unified order God was dispersed everywhere, as a clear and equal radiant intelligibility in which there was no darkness at all. In this new world there

would be no ressentiment or negative emotion, no duplicity and
no appearance-reality contrast. Everything would be immediate
and *present*, especially in the field of human relationships. The
parables and sayings of Jesus were all of them 'eschatological', in
the sense that through them he was attempting to show us what
human relationships would be like in the new world. It would be
an age of reciprocal human transparency in which people would
live generously, from heart to heart.

Meanwhile there was the shock at the end of the old world
to be gone through. It was psychologically traumatic. It was the
death of God, it was nihilism, it was 'the end of the Real' as described by many modern European thinkers from Nietzsche to
Jean Baudrillard. To get through it you needed to return into
the first creation of the world, and to repeat it within yourself,
doing what God had done. You had to muster the creative will
to conquer the ambient universal darkness, choosing light and
projecting out at a world for yourself—a world in which you
can act and express yourself, posit and realise your purposes and
your values.

In the Genesis narrative God is much cheered by the world
he has *carved out* for himself—and so will you be, because God
also *adumbrates* his own future *delegation* (watch the etymology
of all these verbs!) to us of his own creative powers and task.
For God gives to Adam first Eve, who brings him the chance to
create, with her, society and posterity; next, the naming of the
animals whom he will hunt and domesticate; and thirdly, the
Garden, a natural environment that is prepared for the couple
and will support them. These gifts foreshadow a time when humans will become ready to create for themselves—*in the light of*
God.

The main purpose of this chapter has been to persuade you to
adopt a much more *ethical* and *social* understanding of creation
than has been usual amongst Christians since the year 1215. I
need to do this for the sake of my general project, which is to

sketch the completely different and much more advanced religion that Christianity might have become if it had remained closer to the message and the ethics of the original Jesus. During the eighteenth century the *ancien régime* (absolute monarchy, religion-based agricultural civilization) died. God died. Church Christianity died. During the nineteenth century a deeply nostalgic culture-Christianity tried to keep the corpse alive in a state of suspended animation. Today, what remains is melting away so fast that even the popes appear to know the game is up. Indeed it *is*: but at that same moment during the eighteenth century when the old confident dogmatic-metaphysical realism died, the idea was also emerging—in the romantic poets, the new 'legislators of the world', in Wordsworth, and above all in Kant—that we are now the world-builders.[14] From then on the new 'second Christianity' has been slowly emerging.

5

At the End
of the Real

The main purpose of this book is to introduce, and if possible to promote, a long-overdue change in philosophical and religious thought. From at least as far back as Plato, theory has commonly been seen as coming before practice; metaphysics or doctrine has been prior to ethics; and the indicative mood has preceded the imperative. *First* you attempted to gain a general theoretical understanding of reality as a whole and of yourself and your own situation within it, and then *secondly* you turned to ethics, asking 'Within the whole scheme of things as thus described, how should I live? What way or path will best lead me to my own final happiness? And how can I best be reconciled to whatever or Whoever determines the basic conditions of my life and controls my fate?' In political terms, first existing reality was described and justified, and then you were strictly enjoined to adapt yourself to it, or to 'live in accordance with' it.

Such was the customary procedure in a conservative and tradition-directed world which had very little appetite for change. *First* came the general description of the real as a whole, with an account of our place in it, and then *secondly*, an ethic was prescribed, as a way of life appropriate to your station in life. In the West this pattern was followed by the Judaeo-Christian tradition from early times. It is exhibited for example in the Genesis creation myth, where God in the beginning creates the world by reaching out and drawing great lines of distinction that structure the cosmos: between day and night, heaven and earth, land and sea, the sun and the moon, plants and animals, beasts and the first human couple. We have compared God's action here with the way a young girl holding a piece of chalk marks out the playing area for her game of hopscotch. In just the same way, God draws great lines across the primal chaos in order to mark out the playing-field or stage upon which the game of human life is in future to be played. God will then tell the primal couple what, in outline, the game will be; but the whole set-up, having been expressly designed for human habitation, is so benign that at first there needs to be only *one* negative commandment, stating a limit that must not be transgressed. It's there, it seems, as a reminder of something extra that God will also eventually make over to us—but not just yet.

This very familiar background story is enough to remind us that in prescientific times the whole cosmos was generally portrayed as a ready-made, blessed, fixed divine order, invisibly pervaded and governed by divine Providence in every part, and minutely adapted to be our home. Even *after* human disobedience had introduced elements of corruption into the originally-perfect order of things, Creation remained a profound blessing and support for most people, most of the time; so much so that when some great historical disaster destroyed the religious system established in a particular society, individuals could suffer a trauma from which there could be no recovery. The world had become a wasteland, and human life had been emptied of all value.

In Western Europe we have experienced something of all this. The old religion-based agricultural civilization became interwoven with the Greek philosophical tradition (mainly Platonism and stoicism) to develop its own deeply-loved and large-scale ideological self-understanding. Earthly life closely followed its heavenly archetype. Christ enthroned on the firmament of heaven above was a replica of the early Christian Roman emperor, sharing the same halo, vestments and posture. The territorial organization of the church (into provinces, dioceses and so on) copied the organization of the empire. Supporting each other, Christ and Caesar were fused into what we might now call a totalitarian theocracy, which very severely punished heresy and dissent, and levied high taxes to meet its own costs. Yet people loved it and clung to it, both in Eastern and perhaps even more in Western Europe. Bits of it might be absurdly cruel, or irrational, or both, but the old Augustinian Grand Narrative of cosmic creation, fall and redemption lingers yet. In Britain there are still many examples of people who are simultaneously open and even militant unbelievers, and yet also self-declared cultural Christians. Philip Pullman and Richard Dawkins are well-known examples. They like the moral and artistic climate of a post-Christian society, and they recognize that their own moral consciousness is broadly Protestant and Christian-humanitarian. They like Christianity as part of their life's background, and they admire the last monuments of Britain's old Christian culture: the legacy of great mediaeval buildings, the King James Bible, the Book of Common Prayer, and the writings of George Herbert, Milton and Bunyan.

There are dozens of striking examples of the phenomenon that I am briefly sketching. In the Scandinavian countries very few people—even fewer than in Britain—are Christian believers, but most people are firmly loyal to their own country's Lutheran cultural tradition, and the big town churches are very well maintained as symbols of it. People are firmly *post*-Christian, but equally firmly they are post-Christian *cultural* Christians. Their parents or grandparents may have agonized about the loss of the old dogmatic-realist kind of faith, but that's all over now.

Similarly, in music since Verdi and Fauré the requiem has become a popular musical genre that is now quite independent of its original ecclesiastical—and indeed liturgical—setting. A requiem is a concert piece that stands by itself, as indeed does 'religious' music generally. Many composers from Eastern Europe write music that might once have been described as solemn, cosmic and contemplative, and as evoking thoughts of God and life after death. Today it is simply 'religious' in a way that is no longer tied to any particular religious vocabulary or ritual setting.

The churches have not yet decided what they think about cultural Christianity, probably because so many of those who after realism continue to get aesthetic consolation from Christian culture are prominent amongst their own members—and *leaders*, too. Such people know that the old apologetic arguments have all failed, but they do not wish to come out into the open about their own personal lack of strong, or 'literal', dogmatic-realist faith. Nor do they wish to face up to the Death of God and the looming spectre of nihilism. So it is generally more comfortable to stay where one is, as a theologian, a bishop or whatever: to be quietly ironical and not 'come out'. The old ship can sail on for a little longer yet. It is not yet time to take to the lifeboats.

I am not sure about that, though; for there are many indications that the old ship is rotten and is foundering. Biblical criticism has made the story of Christian origins look so murky and confused that it seems very unlikely that the traditional special doctrinal authority of the Bible will ever be restored. Rome is very unlikely ever to find a satisfactory replacement for the neo-Thomist philosophy that it relied upon so heavily between Pope Leo XIII and the Second Vatican Council. Frankly, one cannot see any likelihood of theistic metaphysics and the immortality of the individual human soul being reinstated. No fully-satisfactory new Catholic philosophy is at all likely to appear.

So I am arguing that it is time for some of us to start being courageous. We must leave behind both cultural and ecclesiastical Christianity, admit our emptiness, and struggle for a new beginning. My constructive proposal is that we should learn to see our belieflessness not as a state of being derelict and damned, but as a clean sheet and a challenge to be creative. All the various 'realities' within which human beings have lived in the past—the thousands of different natural languages, cultural totalities and visions of the world—were human creations. We always knew this about visions of the world *other than* our own, and the great gain of learning to think critically is the realization that *our own* philosophical and religious vision and world-view has a human origin and history, and is in no way specially privileged. In the past we thought naively that our God was the one and only true God, whose correct name is known only to us; and that all those other peoples worshipped idols of their own devising. But critical thinking erases that distinction. We are *not* specially privileged. Our God, our language, culture and world-view together comprise a totality that we have evolved within our own past conversation amongst ourselves. Like every other picture that human beings have in the past projected out upon the empty flux of experience, like every other 'reality', it will in the course of time crumble and pass away. Everything, truly everything, pours out and passes away forever. Every 'reality' is always already an interpretation, and so is transient, too, as are we.

At this point, it is vital to stay with this account of universal transience. We do not look for something that supposedly escapes it. On the contrary, we stay with it, and ask if and how we can make constructive use of it.

There are two possible scenarios. One is that we appraise and then actively reject and repudiate existing culturally-established reality. We don't like its values. The world can be and must be reshaped to be much better than this. And if existing reality is irreformable, we must dream up a better world, and then begin moral action to realize it. The other scenario is that for a whole variety of possible reasons a long-established and much-loved reality has begun to fail us. It is decaying, and we who still live in it know that very soon we must leave it and decide for, and start living the life of, a new moral world. The daunting realization, for anyone who finds himself at the end of a world, is that there is no longer any possibility of finding any objective ground for morality. *Everything* is passing away, rapidly, including myself. There is no security, nothing fixed. What can I do?

Moral Faith[15]

(i) Choosing Life

At the end of the last chapter I was recalling the despair of one who has lost all belief in any stable and objective reality or goodness. When I get into such a position I know of nothing other than the empty streaming flux of experience and events, continually pouring out and passing away, and of which my own mortal self is wholly a part. My knowledge is a transient interpretation, imposed upon the flux as the constellations are imposed upon the night sky. Within myself, the flux wells up as *libido*, the life-impulse, a somewhat tangled steam of mixed feelings, struggling to get out into symbolic expression and then passing away. Am I too just a transient interpretation of the flux? Even late in life, when libido is weakening and the fires are dying down, there may still be 'throbbings of noontide', as Thomas Hardy puts it: a brief and almost painful resurgence of the old power of feeling. Then it fades, and again I am left with the thought that, after a lifetime spent in thinking about philosophy, I have only this transient expression that I call myself and my living of my life. If that is all that is now left of me, how can I live, and how can I be happy?

We note here that in the philosophy of life, as in ordinary usage, the word 'life', like the word 'time', has a remarkably wide range of uses.[16] The commonest, perhaps, is that which describes as 'life' the going-on of things in the human social world,

the world of the novel and the newspaper: 'everyday life' and
'London life'. But here we are using the word in a more biological sense. Life is animation, movement, breath, sentience, active
feeling. It is associated above all with *joy*: it turns back upon
itself, feeds upon itself, is enhanced by its own encounters and
exchanges with other manifestations of itself. After a period of
suspended animation or dormancy, it comes back to life, returns
to life, awakens and burgeons. The joys of life, *joie de vivre*, the
Lebensgefühl—in English, 'just the feeling of being alive'. Life's
self-affirmation sweeps all before it.

Everyone who loves natural history will occasionally have
found themselves in an environment crowded with life. In a
field in the Pyrenees, at the end of a hot summer's day, I heard
the sound of millions of stridulating crickets, cicadas and other
insects rising as a loud hum, a roar of joy. Life affirming itself
does not pause to worry about its own brevity and fragility. It
just erupts, and it does not need any supplement. It is sufficient
in itself as a basis for value and happiness.

For almost the whole of the past twenty-five centuries, our
cultural tradition prized theoretical knowledge and understanding above all else, and disparaged the life of transient feeling. You
were enjoined to be passionless, long-termist, prudent and rational. Feeling? It was nothing. Only with Spinoza does philosophy
begin to find a place for the body and the active emotions. Only
with Nietzsche and Lawrence do we at last see the old outlook
getting the savage criticism it thoroughly deserves for being so
poisonous and anti-life. Immediately after Nietzsche, we begin
to see figures such as William James and Albert Schweitzer at last
exploring the possibility of a consistently life-affirming religious
thought and practice.

I am now proposing—as I think most people would—an
even more consistently emotivist philosophy of the self and of
human life and happiness generally: an emotivist view of ethics
and religion, of art, of social life, and even, to a large extent, of

knowledge. Very roughly, what *feels* right, what works *in life*, may be taken for true, *for the present*. That, *that*, is the highest wisdom, and quite good enough for transients like you and me. I am going to be extinct for all eternity rather soon now. I'm only a passer-by; and so are you.

As for the old suspicion, still active as late as Kierkegaard, that the pleasure we feel in life's flow of delicately-differentiated feeling is low-grade, aesthetic, and merely superficial, we may well retort to Kierkegaard, 'What about music; and what indeed about your own love of Mozart?' Music is, in an obvious sense, 'nothing but a flow of sensuous feeling'. But if music can give us no more than a flux of evoked transient feeling, what do you make of the fact that the same small group of German-speaking territories produced almost simultaneously between about 1700 and 1930 traditions of both philosophy and music that are by far the most important in the world?

Suppose yourself to be presented with a choice. You are given the chance to live your life all over again, this time with enough talent to achieve top-level proficiency in one of the three following fields: music, pure mathematics and quantum physics. Which of these three fields would offer you the deepest and most lasting spiritual satisfaction, and would be the best replacement for our now-lost dogmatic-realist religious faith?

I now answer, music. Plato was deeply wrong to privilege detached, passionless, almost bodiless, contemplative reason in the way he did, and particularly so in claiming that it was our best way to happiness. On the contrary, music is all feeling, and music retains a stronger link to religion than any other art has.

Moral Faith

(ii) The Moral Domain

e are talking about an approach to religion and philosophy which has already grasped that all 'realities', political, religious and other, are transient human constructs. When we have reached this point we can consider refusing to accommodate ourselves to presently-established 'reality'. We hope and believe that things could be much better than this. So in both religion and politics we decide to sketch out a 'Dream'—a picture of the way things ought to be, can be, and perhaps one day will be, in the human social world. And we decide to live by the Dream, deliberately *anticipating* it in the hope that (as William James once put it) 'faith in a fact can help create the fact'.[17]

In the case of Gandhi's campaigning on behalf of the Indian minority in South Africa some real success was achieved. Nonviolent but highly persistent civil action to right the wrong of racial discrimination won, in 1914, a promise from the civil power to bring in remedial legislation. This success inspired others also to believe that the old Dream of building a fully-fraternal and supra-ethnic society, the kingdom of God on earth, might be realisable by direct, nonviolent action. In which case we might break with the majority voice of tradition and begin to see religious and moral ideas as *leading* ideas. They don't describe established supernatural facts: their function is to lead us to attempt and even to bring into being something *morally* 'supernatural'; that is, beyond ordinary human nature's present reach. In the past wise old heads had always rebuked youthful idealism by saying that 'You can't change human nature', 'You've got to understand that in the real world such ideas will never be accepted', and 'The reality is that . . .' Now, however, religiously-motivated 'idealism' had achieved a notable success in the supposed 'real' world—as indeed had the anti-slavery campaigns in Britain and France over a century earlier. In which case, religious dreams of a better world may be potent in *creating*, or bringing about, their own realisation. True belief, then, is a dream that we can help to make 'come true', now and in this world.[18]

What sort of dream? It is always contained within certain *parameters*, in the sense that in any human life-world we can imagine our life will remain subject to temporality, contingency and finitude. The one exception, for the present, is that within a few decades we may be discussing the possibility of deferring at least some deaths by genetic engineering of the human genome. This issue has already been discussed by imaginative writers such as Swift and Borges. Their view has been that the prolonged deferral of death would *not* be a blessing. We would after one-and-a-half centuries or so, be sad, hoarsely-whispering ghosts who have badly outlived our own proper lives. We'd be wretched, bored with ourselves and hopelessly bored with life. We would long for extinction: and I agree.

Secondly, the Dream is customarily social, and has a marked-out playing-field in a well-ordered public space—a city, a realm, a domain, a kingdom. The city is in ancient writings pictured as being rich and four-gated, with roads running out from it to link it to all parts of the wider human world. Within the city, human life and communicative relationships are free and immediate to the highest degree, because a number of the great binary contrasts that usually shape human life have been erased.

The distinction between light and shade or darkness is gone, because divinity is dispersed to give a universal, equal light with no shadows or darkness at all.

The distinction between sacred and profane spaces is gone, because the general dispersal of divinity has made all things holy. There is no requirement for any special concentrated presence of the holy in one place.

The distinction between one's public self-presentation and one's interiority is gone, because in this world people are completely frank and transparent, without any duplicity or ulteriority at all. 'What you see' is not just 'what you get': it is all there is. Nothing is, or can be, hidden.

The distinction between short-termism and long-termism is gone because in this world people will already enjoy final happiness now, and have no need to plan any future betterment, either for themselves or for all.

In such a world, the perfect, unconstrained communion of life with life is at its highest, and therefore the general happiness is at its highest by a form of mutual life-enhancement all round. How this happens may be imagined if we recall that the pleasure of attending a concert, a performance, or an exhibition is greatly enhanced if it is *shared*. I think I have never been alone to either a play or concert, because all the best experiences *need* to be shared. The greatest joy in life is always accessed through another life, or through many other lives. For me at least the search for beatitude through solitude is a profound mistake: the self is allocentric, in that it comes to itself, finds itself, recognizes itself and finds its fulfilment through another, or others. Hence the widespread search for love and for recognition by others that we observe today: without the recognition and acceptance of others, the self pines and feels incomplete. Many of our contemporaries have cheerfully given up belief in their own individual life after death, but it is harder to think of oneself as very soon being totally forgotten forever.

Commenting on these views, Etty Hillesum—a Dutch-
Jewish woman, fifteen years older than Anne Frank, who died at
Auschwitz and is now coming to be recognised as a remarkably
gifted and even saintly character—has a remark that reminds us
of her contemporary Simone de Beauvoir: 'Man finds his own
soul through ours'. Thus women find themselves locked into
an instrumental role. When the right one comes along, she
will be for him Universal Woman: indeed, she will be concrete
universal humanity, the *humanum*. He will feel a fully adult and
paid-up member of the human race through her. But who is
she, Etty wonders: she hasn't yet had time to discover who she
is. 'Woman doesn't yet exist as an independent human being',
because she has always been kept too busy being a symbol for her
other, Man. In response to this I suggest one can point out that
since Etty's time, in the early 1940s, women have been spending much longer in education and in becoming established in a
career. They are now taking more time to find themselves before
yielding to the old desire to live for others in the micro-society
of the family. Perhaps they are learning to explore both paths,
and perhaps even have it both ways at once.[19]

Moral Faith

(iii) Coming Out

oth amongst the Greek philosophers and in the Hebrew Bible there was from early times a distinction between the outward appearance which a person presents to the world, and their inner moral truth, often associated with the heart and seen only by God. There is an example in the story of Samuel's selection of David from amongst the sons of Jesse. Eliab is good-looking, but God rejects him, explaining:

> The LORD seeth not as man seeth; for man looketh on the outward appearance, but the LORD looketh on the heart. (1 Samuel 16:76, RV)

An important source of later spirituality is the suggestion here that by turning within, by an act of introversion, we will be able to discover and face up to the truth about ourselves *before God*. The way to the heavenly world is through one's own inwardness: the real you is not the outwardly-presented you, but the inner, hidden you.

The date of that line from 1 Samuel is highly disputable: some might still claim that it goes back to pre-exilic times; others would say that such writing, collecting and working up into a continuous theological narrative the nation's historical traditions as it does, must be of exilic origin; still others would assign it to a date during the Hellenistic period. But however that may be, Aristotle rather similarly distinguishes between a man who merely *appears* righteous, and a man who really *is* righteous 'all the way down' as we might say. Such ideas are very widespread indeed: for example, modern child psychologists, asking how young children develop their first ideas about the mind (what it is, how it works) have concluded that they commonly begin from their experience, both in themselves and in others, of simple cases of *duplicity*, such as 'pretending', or denial of guilt ('I know, but I'm not saying').

In all these cases we seem to be meeting variations of a single theme—the appearance/reality distinction. The public human social world, in which we live and express ourselves, is associated with the realm of fleeting, sensuous outward appearance. To find the deep truth of things we need to pass through or pierce 'the veil of sense' and enter the invisible world of Ideas, a general and timeless Order of Reason which according to Plato is the proper home of your rational soul. In religious language, it is usually spoken of as the world of 'the heart'. To this day young children at primary school are instructed to recollect themselves, to keep still, and to shut out sense-experience. 'Hands together, eyes closed'—and this is how we were taught to pray, and so 'to come to ourselves before God'. For over two millennia in our tradition people were taught—and many are still taught—to contact eternal reality, or God, or the supernatural realm by introversion, by recollecting oneself and 'turning within'. Saints cultivated their own interiority with special zeal. They became strangely amphibian, people who lived in two very different worlds simultaneously—a public life in the common human life-world, and an 'inner life' in 'the interior castle', the many-roomed inner space of the soul. Most mystical language was strongly negative, seeking to draw closer to God by progressively discarding all the human imagery through which ordinary people think of God. In the end one was thinking of God only by unthinking all that is *not* God, until one comes to a featureless emptiness. As Mason's popular hymn puts it:

> Thou art a sea without a shore,
> A sun without a sphere;
> Thy time is now and evermore,
> Thy place is everywhere.

This entire spirituality came to its peak in sixteenth- and seventeenth-century Spain, France, England and the Low Countries. Its last great exponent was Kierkegaard, in whom it is clearly becoming too stressful, and too intellectually-objectionable, to be maintained any longer.

By Kierkegaard's time, Christianity's long, slow turn to this world and this life was already well under way. An extravertive or outward-turning mysticism of the sense of sight, strongly associated with childhood, developed in England from the seventeenth century in religious poets such as Thomas Traherne and Henry Vaughan, and reached an early climax in Wordsworth's *Ode* of 1802, one of the best poems in our language (even if still somewhat marred by residual Platonism). Now the typical movement of the soul is not any longer introvertive (or inward-turning) and towards Unknowing, but extravertive. The real you is now the outwardly-presented you, the social you. The soul is no longer interested in purifying itself and preserving itself for everlasting life in the eternal world, but instead continually *expends* itself, pouring itself out into its own expression, drowning in the visual glory of the world. This extravertive, this-worldly mysticism has some beautiful parallels in Buddhism—especially in Dōgen—and is a striking feature of the oldest available layer of Jesus' Sermon on the Mount. It seems that he too may have been a sunlight-mystic (e.g., Matthew 6:25–30). The light-mysticism is so strong that it makes some of Jesus' language explicitly 'solar'. We are *not* to retire into the darkness of a literal or metaphorical inner chamber, but instead should come out like the sun: we should 'rise and shine' (Matthew 5:14–16, 6:22f.). Thus the self's religious life is wholly this-worldly—another example of Jesus' usually-unnoticed secularism. The self's religious life *consists in* its making itself a purely this-worldly show of itself in self-sacrificial love. Come out, do your thing, strut your stuff! One really is, and feels, happy to die of love, to die into the visual sublime, as in a number of modern artists from late impressionism onwards. We simply do not have time or energy to care about claiming our own rights, or demanding 'justice' or 'closure' for ourselves.

The language is surprisingly strong. In the Platonic-catholic spirituality, someone who had fled away from the world to seek God in a desert hermitage might make himself 'conspicuous by his absence', but in the sayings here under discussion the religious person stands out, conspicuous by his 'ardent' (literally 'burning') *presence*. He's like a standard lamp (Matthew 5:14–16).

Against this background of conspicuous coming-out, we can understand the ethics of excessive generosity. When he is in this mood, the early Jesus (of the tradition up to and including Q) always enjoins excess, chiefly with the object of precluding any lapse into ressentiment, meanness of spirit, and calculation. Let's be clear about this: he who comes out in a fully solar way is definitely not in the least looking for any sort of recognition, or reward or closure. Any kind of personal payoff would utterly subvert this kind of religious life. It is a point which Gandhi grasped very well: the nonviolent campaigner for a moral cause or vision gets the moral force of his campaign entirely from its moral purity and self-expending selflessness.

At this point, solar living is at the opposite pole from traditional Catholicism, which followed Aristotle in endorsing the reward-motive. You put up with austerity now for the sake of a big reward hereafter, the pay-off. But the Jesus-following kingdom-religion I am describing doesn't expect or hope for any kind of payoff hereafter. For me, certainly, just to have been able to express myself and in so doing to pass away forever, is sufficient reward in itself. I want no more than that, and in fact there cannot *be* any more than that. So forget yourself!

Moral Faith

(iv) The Conquest of Pessimism

y early education was steeped in natural science and, from the age of seventeen, the philosophy of Plato. Because of these two influences I was never enthusiastic about miracles or other manifestations of the supernatural. A natural explanation, or perhaps a symbolic interpretation, was always very much more probable. Belief in divinely-caused special interventions into the world-process was surely a sign of naïf eudaemonism and should be systemically downplayed.

Moral faith, by contrast, always comes easily to me. I have in some ways had a hard time, and I have had some very dark periods. But we now recognise that many and perhaps even *most* people have had some experience of anxiety and depression at some period in their lives. This is probably especially true of artists, writers and thinkers. But even people with plenty of experience of personal troubles may yet in the end feel able to say a joyful Yes to life in general and to their own lives in particular.

Wittgenstein near the end was so tense he could scarcely speak, and almost psychotically depressed. But his final message to his beloved friends and students was: 'Tell them I've had a wonderful life!', a movingly-courageous affirmation. Like Tolstoy's Ivan Illych, he got there and was able at the end of his life to say Yes

to his own life. This is moral faith's 'deathbed conversion'; I like
it; it is a great note to go out on.

In my own unimportant case, I was always one of the highly-
visual, with no difficulty at all in loving life, loving the flux of
phenomena, and loving the sight of clouds, insects, birds and
fellow human beings. I always liked humanitarian ethics, and
held to the hope that by piecemeal social reform the social
world could slowly become a kinder and better place. As over
the decades my general philosophical outlook became more anti-
metaphysical and naturalistic, I became more Wittgensteinian
in my wish to affirm the primacy of ordinary life and ordinary
language. I used the slogan: 'God is a secular humanist. If it was
good enough for God to become human in the world and die,
then it should be good enough for you.' Our modern secular
culture may seem post-Christian to many people, but it is also
through and through a product of Christianity. From the outset
it was obvious that Christianity was going to develop in this
direction.

At this point I ask myself: 'What about a rather severe pes-
simist such as Samuel Beckett? Could my ideas have any hope of
appealing to him and perhaps of being helpful to him?'

Beckett is tough. He was in philosophy as least as austere as
Wittgenstein, and had at least as many dark moods. Yet he was
very kind, generous and considerate to friends and to children,
and lived in Paris where he had a very good War, doing useful
work for the *Résistance*. A very good man—but he seems firmly
to have rejected my visual consolations and my religion of life as
sentimental. 'Fuck Life!', says a crippled character in *Rockaby*,
one of the last plays.

What can I say to Beckett? Only, that medical science is making very good progress nowadays, and there is every reason to
hope that before long new drugs and new genetic techniques
may enable us to master the excessive and dark extremes of anxiety and depression that still plague so many humans so much.

Brain chemistry and brain function is one remaining area of life in which our happiness depends upon the working of contingent physical factors about which we presently know too little. To overcome pessimism and restore a person's natural faith in life and love of life may require, not philosophical arguments such as those put forward by William James, but merely a pill. What might Beckett have said to that? Perhaps he might have refused the pill.

I draw the lesson: don't believe depression. Don't suppose that your own black mood, or your own anxiety verging upon panic attacks, is giving you a veridical glimpse of the wretchedness of the human condition generally. It's only a malfunction. Don't trust 'experience', or attempts to derive vital information of a general kind from experience. Instead, trust the general consensus of people in your own period, as it is given by the new idioms coming into use in popular language. Oh, and by the way, the psyche has considerable powers of self-healing. It often recuperates.[20]

Priorities

Language—and especially the English language—
contains very large numbers of antonyms, pairs of
words opposite in meaning to one another. Some
are spatial: up and down, back and front, left and right. Some
are ethical: right and wrong, good and bad.

Another, perhaps even larger group of paired words are often
described as expressing binary contrasts or oppositions, and
seem to reflect the longstanding influence of Plato upon our
culture. They are markedly asymmetrical. The first of each pair
is associated with Plato's world of universal Forms or ideas, and
it is given higher priority or ranking. The second of the pair is
its Other, its shadow or counterpart within Plato's lower world
of transient phenomena. Examples of the contrast are eternity and time, things eternal and things temporal, theory and
practice, the pure and the applied, the contemplative life and
the active life, brainworkers and manual workers, necessity and
contingency, the universal and the singular, the general and the
particular, Reason and sensuousness (including both sense-expe-
riences and sensuous feelings), form and matter, long-termism
and short-termism, recollection and dissipation, and even light
versus shade or darkness. And so the list goes on: one could add
many more of these contrasts without stepping outside Plato's

own language. The most significant—and the hottest—of such additional pairs is surely male and female, because Plato himself has a line describing 'matter and form' as 'the mother and father of being': a line in which he invites the suggestion that our entire culture and construction of the world is an elaboration of the way culture teaches us to understand the difference between the sexes. As is the difference, we may be tempted to continue, between line and colour, melody and harmony, primary and secondary. And it may be added that this suggestion cannot be accused of 'pan-sexualism', for there is a certain pan-sexualism in language itself, for example in the grammatical gendering of nouns in so many languages. English may now lack it, but we do something similar when we speak of a comfortable vessel within which we may be transported around—a car, a ship, an aircraft—as 'she'. For many of us, our first reading of Freud's *The Interpretation of Dreams* was a very effective introduction to the way sexual symbolism pervades our language (while in French, the sexual difference is '*the* difference'). It also permeates much of our slang, too, as one is speedily shown by dipping almost anywhere into Jonathon Green's big *Dictionary of Slang*.

From which remarks we may proceed to state a number of theses that were first well stated by Nietzsche. All our sensations are feelings, and as such they may be pleasant or unpleasant to us. Articulated as language, they are recognizably evaluations. One may say then that delicately-scaled evaluations are ubiquitous in our language. Much of our language is persuasive: we are hoping that you will be in accord with our praisings, recommendations, persuasions and warnings. Indeed, in every culture, people daily quote and maintain—or perhaps are seeking to modify—a large-scale received consensus evaluation of everything, every thing.

All this suggests a picture of ourselves as alert, quivering, highly-tuned animals, instantly responsive to all our sensations. Friend or foe, promise or threat, tasty or distasteful?—we are always evaluating, and language makes our evaluations general, communicable, intelligible. At which point the language of moral evaluation is taking us well along the way to giving us participation in a common *culture*, which has an easily-readable *history*.

Next we begin to notice the way our evaluatively-laden vocabularies discriminate extremely heavily against some groups of people. The outstanding case is that of the commonalty, the *vulgus*, the *plebs*, the masses, the common people, who could not and were not to be taken seriously as individual human beings until the nineteenth (or, you may even think, the *twentieth* century). The common people were low lifes, 'low' as distinct from 'high'. They were almost invariably clownish bumpkins. At their best, they were just the crowded, anonymous 'poor', as contrasted with those who were noble, gentle, liberal, frank and of 'the quality'. People like us. And a similar systematic tilting of vocabulary came into operation against any kind of dissident, whether political, sexual or religious. Language was used, in effect, to police them, and to keep them under control. And the subtlest and most highly-elaborated of all such systems of linguistic discrimination and policing was—and even still *is*—the one that defines women and what society requires of them. The subjection of women was, until very recently, the foundation of culture.

When we realize all this we are coming to the post-Nietzschean period, to the point when we have come to understand what an intolerable jumble our culture is. Many of its prioritizations are objectionable and many of its evaluations are just plain wrong. It is, as Nietzsche very clearly saw, a strange mix of different moral traditions: pagan classical, military, middle-class capitalist, Judaeo-Christian religious, Platonic and other value-scales coexist in confusion. One begins to long for moral simplicity, clarity and integrity. That will be difficult, however, so it would be best to begin by attempting to right a few of the most obvious wrongs.

Moral activism now develops through a series of stages.

At the first stage, I may decide that I can at least do something worthwhile by devoting some of my resources to direct philanthropic action. Such action might (in Britain, for example) involve almsgiving or, on a larger scale, the establishment of an institution such as a block of almshouses, a village school, or a guesthouse for pilgrims, or a hospice. If I am rich enough, I can set up something of this kind without having to change *myself* at all.

Secondly, I may actively campaign on behalf of some neglected and undervalued social group—perhaps by criticizing the derogatory language in which they are commonly spoken of. Such an initiative may develop into a 'cause', which may consume much of a person's life.

Thirdly, I may associate with other like-minded people pursuing other and similar goals, until we realize that we are together turning into something like a political party. Here we are getting closer to religion: and indeed much of the language in which we discuss politics is borrowed from religion. For example, in politics as in religion, we may speak of a creed and a faith, of orthodoxy and dissent, and of conservatives, liberals and radicals. In at least some cases, the degree of commitment required to bring about the promised changes verges upon religion in the intensity of the demand it makes.

Fourthly, I may come to think that even the highest level of political action is not enough. There must be more to life than getting busier and busier, and becoming immersed in more and more detail. In my own moral universe and in my private life I can begin to long for greater moral simplicity, clarity and integrity. But I am *not* here suggesting that we need in our retirement from the fray, the thick of it, to take up the old contemplative life. I am suggesting that we turn to another moral task: the task of learning how to live wholly without ressentiment—even when we are most active.

It is hard to get clear about how much this means: but ordinary, honourable, political struggle makes heavy use of the language of 'fighting'. It divides the world up between allies and enemies. It looks out for rivals. It thinks tactically, strategically. It calculates, it exploits weaknesses, and sometimes it must abruptly abandon an old friend.

Living without ressentiment requires us to give up all that. But when the 'Machiavellian', cunning and combative kind of political infighting is at its most intense and ruthless, we may all of us feel weariness and disgust at being obliged to behave like this. Would it not be better to risk enduring personal suffering for the cause, rather than find ourselves compelled to promote it by these means? And—an important second argument—after we have become accustomed to the very-compromised morality of the period of struggle—when we triumph, when peace comes, we are in any case going to find it very hard to stop the fighting and the dreams of revenge, and go back to being peaceable ordinary citizens. Partisan or guerrilla warfare may be unlovely, but when the fighting is over, the settling of old scores, the public humiliation of perceived collaborators, the greed and the looting are even uglier. It takes a high level of moral integrity to have the strength and the courage to try to stop the hideous excesses that accompany victory in a righteous cause.

The saint longs to be able to live, and to act in a good cause, without any of the great range of negative feelings that are collected under the general label of ressentiment. The saint desires to be able to live and to love the whole world of human life in a purely affirmative and generous way. More nearly than others, Nelson Mandela seems to have succeeded in doing it, during the second half of his life. The good old phrase 'greatness of soul', magnanimity, is the word for it.[21]

The Worth of Everyday Life

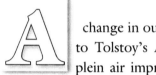 change in our thinking that we generally trace back to Tolstoy's Anna Karenina (1873–77), or to the plein air impressionist painting of Paris during the same decade, sees the greatest achievement of the fully developed Modern age as being its very strong affirmation of the intrinsic value and interestingness of ordinary people and ordinary everyday life. I think first of Levin working in his fields alongside the peasants, and of a marvellous Edouard Manet canvas that depicts workmen digging up a Paris street on a hot sunny day. Paris is paradis. Modern sanitation had recently made cities tolerably healthy to live in for the very first time, and the income of an ordinary urban worker was beginning to be sufficient to allow a little leisure, and perhaps an excursion in a rowing boat, or by railway train. So for the first time in history it becomes possible to take a serious interest in, and to affirm the value of the ordinary lives of ordinary people. Before long it will be possible for an individual poor person to become the central character in a novel.

—Or is there perhaps something of a tour de force here? Can one be completely happy in secular ordinariness, just sitting in the sun on the riverbank; or is this secular ordinariness—newly unsupported by any religious or similar ideology as it is—is it a fragile mask, covering an imminent collapse of value and a spiritual desert? At the time many critics found the innocent secularism of the impressionists alarming. But early American art collectors who bought the paintings liked their democratic ordinariness; and so do most of us now.

To get a clearer view of the issue here, we need briefly to attend to the history of ordinariness.

Ordinariness, from Latin ordo, implies the quiet following of a customary routine. Ordinary days are ferial days, unmarked by any appointed religious observance such as a feast or a fast. Idiomatically, ordinariness is 'nothing special': it is unremarkable, unnoticeable, undistinguished, nondescript and generally forgettable, there being nothing extraordinary, or out of the ordinary about it. Mainly because in a crowded world things don't get seen unless they are notable, ordinariness is anonymous to an astonishing degree. Consider the profound anonymity of the poor in Thomas Gray's celebrated Elegy Written in a Country Churchyard. For the poet, it's just a fact, and he somehow cannot imagine it being otherwise. He even quite likes the idea of disappearing into their anonymous mass himself when he dies and is buried amongst them. Till then, he is one of the gentlefolk who briefly picked up poets such as Robert Burns and John Clare, toyed with them, didn't know quite what to do with them, and then tossed them aside and completely forgot them. It was simply not possible two centuries ago for a gentleman to treat someone from the masses, or the common people—even someone talented—as an individual fellow-human. The gentleman was classy and the ordinary man was not: in those days they distinguished 'the classes' from 'the masses', and it was only with industrialization that the common people at last decisively asserted themselves, developing for themselves representative organizations, leaders and a new class name, 'the working class', that in due course was able to force recognition of itself—a long struggle, and not over yet.

Thus a long, long history in our culture still makes ordinariness seem vague, forgettable and uninteresting. To attract any attention or have any merit, it seems that you need to be a bit classy, a bit different. You need to be notable, to stand out. The general run of things is boring, sleepy, monotonous.

Four lines of argument will show us the way out of this difficulty.

First, there is no purely objective reality, meaningfulness, truth or value. What gives the world interestingness, colours it up, and makes things precious is our own streaming libido pouring out of us and onto the various objects of our attention: the magical shimmer of phenomena, other life, replies to our signals. Much of this is a matter of education: we can learn the more active use of our eyes and ears, and we can learn to love life every day. Education can and should vastly enrich perception and feeling.

Secondly, and developing the same point, we can learn to live without any ressentiment or negative feeling. Solarity, the highest degree of emotional expressiveness, is learnable. For example, you can pick up the telephone right now, and make contact again with that person from whom you have been estranged for many years. Do it: have just a cool and friendly conversation, and afterwards you will find yourself feeling better (note the word 'feeling') for the rest of the day. The negative emotions tangle and block the flow of our feeling for life. If one by one, we remove the blockages, we get an almost immediate enhancement of our feeling for life. Solar living becomes gradually more easy and habitual. It becomes easier to be more outgoing.

Thirdly, we need to retrace the arguments (many of the best of them can be found in Wittgenstein, who was himself a strong Tolstoyan) for treating ordinary language and ordinary life as basic for the whole of human philosophy. The exceptional human being, that is, the creative genius, the highly-productive scientist and the saint, are never people who have entirely left

ordinariness behind them. On the contrary, ordinariness is like
an old farmhouse, and a highly-developed personal talent is like
a modern offshoot or lean-to extension added on to it. The offshoot can't stand alone. It isn't complete enough. It still needs
the old building's support.

An oddly-vivid example of the way we cannot become totally
independent of ordinariness is given by St Anthony of Egypt
(251?–356), who was the first and best known of the desert
solitaries. It is well known what he found life in the desert very
tough. Demons assailed him; but according to the standard
biography, the Vita Anthonii, he found comfort and strength
by returning to the memory of his mother and sister. Even
Anthony, in his strange and perhaps pathological pursuit of an
almost crazy way of life, found that he couldn't entirely do without human normality.

The fourth argument points out that close examination of
the evolving idioms of ordinary language will soon convince us
that ordinary language, being an ancient communal product,
is much quicker and cleverer, and even much deeper than we
individuals are. This realization is rather recent. In the great
Oxford English Dictionary (1884–1928) the use of words is il-
lustrated by citations from canonical English writers. Idiomatic
phrases in popular use were commonly thought of us 'clichés',
and as uninteresting. But many of the keenest buyers and users
of dictionaries nowadays are people who are learning English as a
foreign language (EFL), and they need to have advance warning
of many of the most striking idioms. So it is that a great many,
perhaps nearly all, of the new dictionaries published in the past
twenty-five years or so list large numbers of idiomatic phrases.
When at the end of the 1990s I was writing my own little studies
of religious and philosophical thought in our everyday speech,
I was directed to these books as useful sources from which to
begin making my own collections of idioms. I was soon obliged
to recognize how surprisingly up-to-date, sophisticated and

forceful many idioms are. Perhaps if you are sleepless tonight, you may care to think about the use of the word 'it' in phrases such as It is hot today (African version: God is hot today), It came to pass, Loving it, Don't let it get you down, Face up to it, and It befell upon a day. If you get really hooked, you will reach for a pen and paper, and have several hundred phrases by breakfast-time. Winding and irregular, like the lanes at the heart of an ancient city centre, ordinary language is much thicker and deeper than we used to realize. In your collection you will find idioms a thousand years old (like it is hot) sitting quietly next to idioms only twenty years old (are you up for it?).

We return to the main line of argument with the general remark that ordinary language, and ordinary life, are not, or do not have to be as banal as many unobservant people think. Everything depends upon the intensity and the solar whole-heartedness with which you commit yourself to it—and to ordinary people, too. Wittgenstein used to urge his students to give up philosophy and return into full-time ordinariness by becoming, for example, shop assistants. I will not go as far as that, but I do think that if we can learn to be solar and live wholly without ressentiment we will find that ordinariness can be unexpectedly satisfying.

12

Living the Dream

Throughout this book we have been contrasting two very different logics of religious teaching.

The first is that followed by traditional western Christianity. It is dogmatic-realist, presenting an account of the cosmic situation in which we humans find ourselves. It includes a briefly-described metaphysics of God, the world, and the human self which is seen as being an immortal rational soul. It then sets out a very large-scale narrative of cosmic Creation, Fall and Redemption, ending with an account of faith and of the Church as offering us a way to eternal salvation in the heavenly world after death. The Christian life was then described under two headings, worship and ethics, which together presented a rational human response to the remarkable news of all that God had done for us and for our salvation. The great narrative is undoubtedly to be understood in a realistic way, because one cannot allegorize away its emphasis on the way God has acted first, before we had acquired any merit at all. Similarly, the old belief in salvation after death must also be understood realistically or it cannot function as a reward or recompense.

Up to the time of René Descartes—and even, it may be said, up to the time of Locke, Leibniz and Berkeley, around the first quarter of the eighteenth century, most of the major European

philosophers still presented their teaching in broad agreement
with the Christian metaphysics of God, the world and the soul.
But by the end of the eighteenth century the leading philosophers were moving outside the Christian tradition, and today
it is quite clear that they are not coming back. Similarly, the
old grand narrative which Reformed preachers used to call the
'Plan of Salvation' faded away and died on a timeline about
fifty years later. When around 1840 the last major Christian
thinker, Kierkegaard, read the Young Hegelians—including
David Friedrich Strauss and Ludwig Feuerbach—he could see
that the game was up. Like many others, Kierkegaard retreated
to Christian ethics, the last stronghold so far as traditional apologetics was concerned. But this retreat to ethics implies a tacit
abandonment of all supernatural doctrine.

In traditional Christianity you were assured that the universe
is an absolute monarchy ruled by a King who is unbounded in
his power, his justice and his mercy. You deserve damnation, but
he offers you forgiveness and a path to eternal happiness in the
light of his presence. Accept the offer, worship him, and live the
life.

In the Middle Ages, the Latin Church, whose Patriarch was
the Bishop of Rome, taught that the truth of the propositions of
faith was metaphysically certain. To question and to deny any of
them was a very grave crime that might be punishable by death.
The English theological master Richard Hooker recognized that
amongst devout readers of scripture there may be serious differences of interpretation. Accordingly he said only that the truth
of the propositions of faith is morally certain. Moral certainty is,
as the phrase goes, "enough to go on" in a practical matter. But
today, after a truly enormous increase in our critically-established
and tested knowledge in the fields of both natural science and
human history, we now know for sure that almost none of the
propositions of faith is testably and straightforwardly true. In the
Apostle's Creed, it is quite probably true that Jesus lived, was

'born of Mary, suffered under Pontius Pilate, (and) was cruci-
fied, dead, and buried'. Otherwise, it is frankly not surprising
that hostile critics should regard the entire doctrine-system as a
fairy-tale. By today's standards, it is.

In the modern period, the major Protestant churches have, in
varying degrees, distanced themselves from their own classical
confessions of faith, which are now regarded as being expressed
in the vocabulary of the period or periods when they were written. 'We wouldn't put it quite like that now', it is said, and the
offending form of words is 'put on the back burner', in a place
where it can quietly fade away. It is not brought to light, but
nor is it openly contradicted: it is simply left under wraps, like
furniture in the old family home which the old couple have no
use for at present. Maybe one day they will get it out again, and
maybe not.

An example is the old cycle of dogmas about purgatory, the
treasury of merit, and indulgences. These dogmas were never
formally revoked, but you may be pretty sure that no modern
pope is likely to wish to revive them.

Today the old doctrine-system is something of a museum
piece. An old maxim ran: 'The Church to teach, and the Bible
to prove', but today no careful student of the New Testament
would say that it attests the truth of orthodox Christian doctrine. In fact, only two major doctrines were ever defined in
detail at church councils, the dogmas of the Trinity and of the
Incarnation, and both go well beyond anything that can be cited
from the New Testament in support of them. In several areas,
including the atoning death of Christ and life after death, no
morally-attractive and moderately-credible accounts have ever
been given. All that can be said today is that there are still some
realistic theists for whom the heart of dogmatic faith is confi-
dence in the objective reality of God's goodness and almighty
power, exerted to create and sustain us, and then also to save us
from our sins. Although many of the details are nowadays hazy,

such people still maintain that faith, worship and the practice of Christian ethics is always a response on our part to the prior action of God.

With that in mind, we turn now to the alternative and, as I have called it, 'ethics-led' account of religious belief for today. You may be reminded of the Rev. Dr Martin Luther King's celebrated speech in the year 1963 at Washington DC, as you read what follows here:

> Morally, much in our life and in our social world seems to us to be unacceptable. In many respects human relations are far below what they should be. Indeed, many things need to be turned upside-down. We need a revolution in our values.
>
> I have a Dream that the better world we long to see can come, must come, will come soon.
>
> Join me.
>
> Let us together live the Dream.
>
> We can and eventually we will make it come true.

This minimal, rather skeletal account may remind you of a number of other figures whose names we have already mentioned—Mandela, Gandhi and in particular the Jesus of the Synoptic Gospels (Mark 1:15, Matthew 4:17, Luke 4:43). Individual teachers may differ in the details of what is wrong with the present human world and what a better world would look like. Some hope that it will come through a period of revolutionary upheaval, while others give us an active role and debate the techniques we may use in our campaigning for a better world. But they are all agreed upon some essential points.

They will agree that commitment to live the Dream is highly self-involving. You have to be self-critical about your own aims and motives, about the goals you are seeking, and about the methods you may use in pursuit of them.

Secondly, whereas in the old realist-dogmatic account God acts first and in the end does everything because human action cannot change anything deep, in many of the new ethics-led accounts of it all we humans do everything. The "ethical dream" interpretation of religious belief thus becomes independent of any supernatural support or backing.

Thirdly, when we are talking of the Dream and living the Dream, we are not talking merely of preserving or reviving some venerated ancestral way of life that is threatened by secular modernity. Examples of this might be the biblical Rechabites who lived in tents and avoided alcohol, or the American Mennonites who rather similarly preserve a pre-scientific agricultural way of life in the United States today. Nor are we talking about single-issue campaigners, however estimable, such as the UK-based Howard League for Penal Reform. No: we are talking in a totalizing way about an entire world-view that includes everything. Realists put some supernatural theology in front of their ethics: non-realists do not. They start with their ethical dissatisfaction and their demand. In this sense Paul was a theological realist and Jesus was not. In the case of Jesus an ethical approach to religion becomes so powerful that it comes to deal with the rejection of an old world and the building of a new. On my account, we and our language are always alone, and we make it all. We can know of no 'real' world other than 'our' world. The only world we can call real is a world that we can accept ethically.

Fourthly and finally, mainstream ecclesiastical Christianity always tended to put worship first, and ethics a very bad second. For example, the Benedictines reduced Christianity to the cult, with ethics reduced to the self-purification needed if the cult was to be performed as it should be. In accordance with that tradition, modern Christianity is often little more than churchgoing with small-scale almsgiving. But in our ethics-led, 'Dream' interpretation of religious thought and life, ethics comes first, really first, as it did, for example, in the case of Jesus himself. The gospels do not exactly portray him as either a zealous ascetic or a 'churchgoer'.

◆ ◆ ◆

The obvious question to which we have been leading up must now present itself. Are the Western-tradition churches now going over rapidly to the ethics-led, 'Dream' point of view? They all seem quite recently to have put the whole of orthodox doctrine on the back burner, where it is neither exposed to the light or criticized, but is simply quietly left without comment. In practice the churches now confine themselves to current practical issues and controversies, problems of recruitment, government, corruption and reform, and to treating the major feasts as the occasion for uplifting moral allegorizing. Journalists go along with this: at press conferences they ask questions only about current practical and moral questions.

Only sixty-five years ago, things were very different. On 1 November 1950 Pope Pius XII, in *Munificentissimus Deus* proclaimed the dogma of the Corporal Assumption of the Blessed Virgin Mary into heavenly glory, and the faithful were delighted. This was the last preposterous affirmation of extreme dogmatic realism, affirming bodily life in a local heaven up in the sky, in total disregard of any advances in cosmology since the Middle Ages. Think about it: as in the case of Jesus, if someone is to ascend and sit in a bodily heaven in the sky, God must presumably supply artificial gravity, the correct mix of nitrogen and oxygen, and of course a tasty vegetarian diet (see, for example, Isaiah 65:25; there can be no meat-eating in paradise).

Things have changed since 1950, and especially during the past thirty years or so since the Second Vatican Council. Recognition at Rome itself of the new situation was delayed by the extreme conservatism of Pope John Paul II, who had spent most of his life in the intellectually-sheltered culture of Eastern Europe under Communist Party rule. He continued throughout his life to use the vocabulary of St Thomas Aquinas as if it still made sense—though one should also say that he was painfully aware of being acutely constrained by his institutional role. He couldn't ever speak or write as a free individual—while around him people were aware of intellectual disarray in the seminaries, and of a chasm between much of the ethical teaching of the hierarchy and the actual beliefs and practice of the laity.

After John Paul II's death, the new Pope Benedict in a public lecture called for Catholic theologians and philosophers to give their attention to the problem of faith and reason. A cri de coeur, confirmed by the fact that his own big book about Christ failed because it had to deny and disregard elementary facts about the gospels that are known to every first-year theology student.

It seemed that the Church was intellectually bankrupt and irreformable. Like the Protestant churches but even more so, Rome was stuck in an extreme form of dogmatic realism which could come to terms neither with the philosophy of Kant nor with the modern critical way of reading an historical text. Nor could it respond to rapid cultural change, or to the acute difficulty of keeping anything secret in the all-exposing media age.

But then, just when it seemed that reform and renewal were no longer possible, Pope Francis emerged in 2013. With him came a sudden and remarkable change of atmosphere. All the usual journalists wrote tens of thousands of words about it, but not one grasped the philosophical shift that the new pope seems to have made. Broadly, you do not get to be pope unless you are bright enough to know the score, and I have no doubt that both Benedict, the present Pope Emeritus, and Pope Francis understand very well the seriousness of their church's intellectual situation, as well as the obviously declining numbers and morale of both secular priests and members of religious orders.

One apologetic text by Francis is in the public domain as I write.[22] The document emanates from the Vatican, which indicates that Pope Francis circulated his own draft to at least some colleagues for comment and advice, and therefore that no powerful person or group sought to stop it. It is cautiously worded in a somewhat-flowery style; but to the careful reader it indicates something of Francis' philosophy of religion.

We notice first that the old Aristotle-and-Aquinas vocabulary is wholly gone, and that Francis says nothing that must be interpreted as strictly implying belief in metaphysical realism. Instead, his language is symbolic and his argument is entirely ethical. But lest you should think he actually agrees with me, in detail, I must hasten to point out that for him 'the Dream' is not the kingdom of God, but simply the whole concrete lived life, experience and action of the Church. Living within that Dream I can—presumably metaphorically—'encounter Christ' and via him be given an idea of what I myself ought to become. Dr Scalfari, to whom Francis writes, has challenged Francis to come to terms with the historical Jesus, but Francis—although he does go so far as to acknowledge that Mark is nowadays regarded as being the earliest of the gospels—does not distinguish the historical Jesus from the Christ of faith. For him the Jesus of the gospels, who is already highly theologized, is the 'real' Jesus, both of history and of faith. Thus Francis, rather startlingly, has gone about as far along with me as I could possibly expect of him, and nobody is going to be asking: 'Is the pope a Catholic?' What is startling and refreshing is that he goes as far as he does in dropping the traditional metaphysical and dogmatic realism and giving a 'Franciscan', that is, a more ethical and humanistic account of the life of faith.

At a very late stage I subjoin a reply to an objection. In his long eighteenth and last paragraph, Francis states that 'God is reality with a capital "R"'. Is he leaving room for a possible reintroduction of metaphysical realism? No, because in the surrounding sentences he has spelt out a thoroughly ethical account of truth. 'Truth is a relationship', he says: 'it is given to us always and only as a way and as a life.' This means that for him truth is trustworthiness, reliability and moral constancy. Which means: 'Stick to your religious values, and they will not let you down.

You will survive: you will come through.' Once again, I am startled and shocked to see how little Francis differs from me. For him it seems that ethics really does come first. It determines religious truth.

13

Dreaming Up

I t is impossible not to admire the energetic start Pope Francis has made, even though he begins his reign at an advanced age. He clearly knows the score, and is doing all he possibly can to restore at least something of Christianity's intellectual and moral credibility. He is an honest man who has quietly dropped a vast amount of dead vocabulary, dead philosophy and dead apologetic argument. In the spirit of Francis of Assisi, he has shifted in the direction of affirming all-out the priority of ethics in general, and the teaching of Jesus in particular. This implies a shift away from a law-governed, rational, long-termist vision of life towards short-termism, simplicity of life and fresh, spontaneous *disponibilité* (Gabriel Marcel's word for openness and ready availability to others). He gives the impression of preferring to live not in palatial seclusion, but out of doors amongst ordinary humanity. He prefers spontaneous feeling to prudent calculation.

Where I must, however, part company with him is over his (of course, unavoidable) commitment to a very high, catholic understanding of the Church. Originally, the Church was a temporary organization set up as a night watchman, to keep vigil during the time of waiting for the promised kingdom to be set up on earth by Jesus on his return. The Church gradually developed a rich theology of itself. It was the new Israel; it was one

91

of a pair of beautiful sisters, the Church and the Synagogue; it
was a new Temple, founded upon Jesus Christ and his apostles;
it was a body, the Body of Christ; it was an army on the march
through the wilderness of this world and this life, and led by
the leading bishops, the successors of the apostles. It was even
a kind of territorial empire, the spiritual ghost or shadow of the
Roman Empire. The Church was believed to be founded upon
and sustained by a number of promises and guarantees given to
it by Christ, and as its own self-understanding grew ever more
exalted the Church became cosmic. It saw itself as advancing
from being the Church Militant to being the Church Expectant,
and finally the Church Triumphant in heaven. Through the gift
of the keys of the kingdom to Peter, the Church swallowed the
kingdom of God whole, and almost deified itself. Its formalized
doctrine was immutable, its teaching was infallible, it was indefectible and so on.

All this extravagant rhetoric came to something of a climax
in the Bull *Unam Sanctam* of 1302, in which Boniface VIII
asserted the jurisdiction of the pope over all creatures. Against
such a background, an ordinary priest who had the power to
celebrate Mass was a being greater than a king.

Clearly much of this hyperbole is on the back burner nowadays, and has been so at least since Vatican II in the 1960s. But
it has left its mark upon Catholics, who, a little like Muslims, are
still apt to think that their own religion is the only serious form
of religion in existence, so that outside it there is nothing. Thus
it may well be that for Francis the Church is still the Dream itself embodied and established on earth. The Church can inspire,
nourish, and satisfy all our aspirations. It can take us all the way.

As it is for other protestants (and especially for Luther and
Kant), the Dream is, for me, a spiritual ideal of perfection that
can perhaps never quite be fully realized on earth. We dream that
it may be possible to live entirely without ressentiment in a fully
reconciled, co-operative, face-to-face society. We dream of a life

lived wholly for love. The Dream functions to make us dissatisfied with present ethical reality, both in ourselves and around us. It functions as a 'leading idea', raising our expectations and always ahead of us. In religion and ethics, as in education, far too many people's aspirations are set far too low. What they need is not a God who actually exists, but a God-ideal of perfection that awakens and energizes them, making them desire constantly to project out and to realize a better world than this one. A God who actually exists would be merely an ideological justification of present reality. Fortunately, he doesn't actually exist and, by the way, the cosmos is not run as a benevolent absolute monarchy.

In sum, non-realism plus dancing with the Dream is true religion, whereas realism about God is, in Kant's words, 'dogmatic slumber', an idle satisfaction with present reality.

How do we dream up the Dream? The best illustrations date from ancient pre-philosophical times, when people naturally and readily projected out mythical fulfilments of their urgent hopes. The three chief stories are, in the first place, The Last Battle. Here, ordinarily people experience in their own lives a seemingly endless struggle between good and evil powers, in which they themselves are pawns. They dream of a last battle, won by the good party, after which will follow a long age of peace and plenty. Israel seems to have learnt from an early Iranian version of this myth.

Secondly, there is The Last Judgement. Ordinary people often feel unrecognized and unjustly treated, and long to see an authoritative, public and final vindication of the innocent and righteous poor. The theme of a Last Judgement is found in virtually all the world's major religious traditions, often amalgamated with the old philosophical dream of a blessed revelation of final truth at the end of time.

Thirdly, there is the more directly-political dream of a Revolutionary Turning Upside-down of the whole existing social order and its values. As a red-letter saying attributed to Jesus has it: 'The first will be last, and the last first'. With this, may be combined the theme of the Remnant. The elect people may have suffered catastrophic defeat and exile, which has greatly reduced their numbers. But this remnant will return singing, they will rebuild their ruined City, and the sound of children playing will again be heard in its streets. Here the main emphasis is not upon the open publication of objective truth and vindication of objective goodness at the end of history, but rather upon the universal restoration (technically, apokatastasis) of so many lost and forgotten lives and hopes.

All these stories are, by top standards, obvious fantasies and illusory wish-fulfilments—as Plato himself clearly recognizes. They are myths, and not quite a part of philosophy; but they do remind us of why ordinary people under pressure have always instinctively opted for an ethics-led approach to religious thought. Ordinary people's deep dissatisfaction with their lot is in the end an ethical dissatisfaction with existing reality.

But there is of course no such long-term remedy as the myths propose. Everything is contingent, everything is transient, and even if the human race contrives to live on for thousands of years, people will never see any final vindication, public exhibition, and enthronement of either objective reality, objective truth, or objective goodness. The very nature of language shows that all these things are perpetually contested and never finalized. Everything is transient; even ourselves and our dreams. We need the Dream to live by, but it is just that . . . a dream.

Hence I insist on the need for the Dream to give us, and perpetually to raise, our expectations and our hopes. But I insist that there is no finalization, and therefore that there is no alternative for us but joyful affirmation and acceptance of our own transience, and all-out solar, self-expending, living. Consciousness is raised, and our feeling-life is made yet more poignant by our continuing love for a God who died in the eighteenth century and has now become lifted into ideality, an impossible Dream that forever drives us on and eludes our grasp.

Where did I first learn this idea? At school, in about 1950, and from Robert Browning's poem 'A Grammarian's Funeral'. On religion, Browning is the best of the Victorian poets.[23]

Without
Consolation

hen he discovered the philosophy of the Hindu Upanishads, which somewhat resembles his own German idealism, Schopenhauer clung to it: 'It has been the consolation of my life', he declares—making me wonder why philosophers from the ancient sceptics and Boethius to Hume and Russell have so often spoken of the comfort to be gained from the study of philosophy. Whereas religion is usually relatively 'hot'—ranging, as it does, from extreme guilt and fears that one is careering downwards into eternal damnation, to a joyful confidence in one's own final salvation—philosophy by contrast is praised for being so calm and cool.

This may be partly because the territory of philosophy is very sparsely populated: you may well find yourself living entirely alone and never meeting a kindred spirit. More often, sceptics say that religious dogmatism is too fierce and violent, and that it is a great comfort to flee from it into the sceptical philosopher's uncommitted suspension of belief and tranquillity or serenity of mind (ataraxia). Hume, who escaped from Calvinist religion into the 'mitigated scepticism' of a great philosopher, is particularly strong on this point.

More generally, is there not almost everywhere an underlying agreement that most of us privately find the human condition pretty bleak? Early on in life, a child that is loved can somehow play and be happy in almost any circumstances, but in adulthood we too often find ourselves struggling to keep up our own morale in the face of disappointments, misfortunes and, above all, the long, long downward slope to an often very ignoble end, in which we are finally lost and quickly forgotten. Is it not true that most people's lives start well, or, to put it more cautiously, that it is quite easy to give the vast majority of human beings a happy start in life, but our extended modern lifespan ensures that in our middle and later years most of us face a long decline, with at least a few very hard knocks along the way. Against this general background understanding, we may see both philosophers and people of religion as marketing consolatory visions in their very different ways.

At least some writers declare that it is their duty to help to make ordinary people's lives bearable. The liberal protestant philosopher of religion John Hick always saw the hope of a blessed life after death as the ordinary person's theodicy. We have to be able to expect a life after death happy enough to compensate us for this life's disappointments and sufferings, if we are to continue to believe in the goodness of a realist God—who after all has inflicted those same sufferings upon us. Hick was, almost to the end, a strong theological realist, who in his nineties would begin arguing vehemently with me as he opened his front door when I went to see him. I would fight back: 'You picture God as contemplating the Holocaust with equanimity as it was occurring, because he knows that he'll put it right for those Jewish people later on? You picture God as contemplating the suffering of Christ on the cross, and doing nothing about it because in the end he himself will make that suffering make sense?' At the end of his life Hick slightly shifted his position by giving up belief in the personality of God. His God became something more like Brahman. But he still thought that he must cling to metaphysical realism in order to keep alive a vision of It All as 'making sense'—as being in the end morally tolerable and intellectually coherent. It was necessary to believe in the objective unity of the

Real and the Good, and to maintain the hope that after death we will somehow find the intellectual and moral satisfaction that has eluded us in life.

I cannot offer that much. I can and do argue that the non-realist God, being simply a pure spiritual ideal, is not to be blamed for the many evils that threaten us, and is certainly not one who offers rewards in the next life in the hope of persuading us to stick it out in this life. The realist God is morally ugly; the non-realist God is a pure spiritual ideal of freedom, clarity and spiritual perfection. He is 'the Pearl of Great Price' but not a being, and therefore is religiously-speaking a huge advance on the realist God of the past. He is no longer our Alpha, our first cause, because all that has been handed over to science; but he then becomes much more clearly and purely our Omega, our chief End.

But he does not offer any consolations. We are alone. As the greatest of non-realists, Spinoza, puts it: 'He who loves God must not expect to be loved back'. Does that matter?

I think not. For the non-realist the human self is a complex process, a role on life's stage, and a cluster of interpretations. We act it out and in the end simply expend it. We don't have to worry about keeping our souls free from pollution by sin, nor about the dangers of 'selling one's soul'. The self just does not have to be worried about. We can let it go, as in the end we must. It's a curiously difficult doctrine to communicate, but the anatta doctrine, that there is no core-self, is unexpectedly liberating and joyful. Do you mind? I don't mind at all. And always watch the uses of that verb 'to mind': it interestingly links thought with worry, care, Sorge.

In the past, in our monotheistic group of traditions, realistic and interventionist theism has often led us to become too preoccupied with our own inwardness—precisely because our inwardness was seen as being always wide open to the silent gaze of God, and perhaps also open to invasion by finite spirits, angels and demons, fighting against each other for control of us and of our fate. A *bellum intestinum* was going on all the time, and we are reminded that the literary form of allegory was first invented and developed during the very period when the early Christians were developing their own ideas about spirituality, religious selfhood and the religious life. Not surprisingly, the idea developed that the best life must be one in which a large part of one's time is spent in solitary self-examination and battles for self-mastery. Your first task as a Christian was to win the fight against yourself.[24]

Many years ago (at least fifty) I read in H. J. Davis's large multivolume *Moral Theology*, a solemn discussion of what the confessor should say to a penitent who had inadvertently swallowed a little toothpaste while engaged in his or her Sunday morning ablutions. Did this amount to a breach of the pre-eucharistic fast? I remember thinking in my usual insolent way that I must surely distance myself considerably from any such way of thinking, and all the metaphysical and religious ideas that had given rise to it. Now, all these very troubled years later, I can claim to have done so, in spite of a lengthy period of devotion to Kierkegaard. Now I see that our inwardness is not constantly wide open to invasion by a host of warring supernatural beings and influences. On the contrary, what there is of it is quiet, is our own, and is (if we are lucky) not very interesting. Our true 'selfhood' or 'personhood' is 'theatrical': it is realized, not by recollection and introversion, but by extraversion, by going out into symbolic expression and communication with other people. The self is simply to be expended. When it's gone, so are we. Meanwhile the true religious happiness is simply our present joy in going out into expression, communication, tending, work and creativity. Do your thing, strut your stuff, put on a good show, live as intensely as you can in the present moment. There is nothing else: there couldn't be. To realize this is to have finally outgrown any need for consolation.

15

Without
Reward

D uring the five millennia or so of religion-based agricultural civilization, between the early Bronze Age and the beginnings of modernity, people tended to see both the earthly city here below and its counterpart, the heavenly city in the world above, as absolute monarchies governed by law. If you were in dispute with a fellow-citizen, the legal system provided you with an opportunity to appeal to the king, or to some judge acting in his name, for arbitration and justice. For example, the king might grant regular audiences by standing at the gates of the city as people daily passed through them on their way to and from work; or he or his deputy might be available at a Stone of Judgement; or the king might sit enthroned with his ministers on either side of him in the basilica, or royal audience-hall.

But now suppose that your deep feeling of moral discontent arises not just at the social level, but at a level that can only be called 'cosmic'. There is something morally disappointing, or frustrating, or even outrageous about the human situation generally. Natural and political disasters, personal misfortune and tragedy threaten us all the time, and eventually old age, sickness and death await us all. The unjust afflictions of the righteous poor, who are severely oppressed by the rich and powerful, but have no remedy, creates a particularly strong cosmic demand for moral justice. Why is there not . . . no, surely there must be a great and final Assize presided over by God, or by his right-hand man, at which the accounts are balanced and people will get their deserts. The afflicted righteous receive the reward they deserve, and the wicked who got away with it in this life will receive the everlasting punishment they thoroughly deserve.

So strongly is all this felt that the belief in a Last Judgement is probably the single most widely-held of all religious beliefs. For example, the blindfolded figure of Justice and the scales with which she weighs and assesses the merits of human souls, that today stands above the Central Criminal Court (the 'Old Bailey') in London is actually derived from Ancient Egyptian tomb-paintings.

Another, even stranger, example: despite the firmly-entrenched moral principle in Christianity that we should be, as God is, endlessly generous, loving and forgiving even to those who have trespassed against us, Christian writers in the Middle Ages continued to insist that we should look with moral satisfaction at hell and at what goes on there. John Bunyan's *Mr Badman* (1680) is one of the last solidly-Christian writings—and one of the first to shed a tear over a reprobate.

The whole story illustrates a sense in which, in the past, religious thought has often purported to be ethics-led—but with gruesome results. For around the world lurid and, one has to say, perverse and sadistic depictions of the torments of the damned are found in all major religious traditions. All of which creates a difficulty for me. For me, an ethics-led religious thought is a strong desire to live, so far as one can, entirely without all the negative emotions that I gather under the label 'ressentiment'. Unfortunately, the whole doctrinal story of a Last Judgement and a final condemnation of the wicked is clearly inspired by ressentiment, and is not truly moral at all. It all too vividly reminds us of those people, nowadays, who crusade for 'justice', declaring that they will not have 'closure' until they have seen some-body suffer. For them, justice is merely revenge. But in my view we should not allow any place for such feelings in our hearts. On the contrary, we should try, as far as we can, joyfully to affirm and to commit ourselves to the world's utterly transient beauty; and we should try to live by love only.

In order to preserve these doctrines from corruption it is vital that we see ourselves as living now in the kingdom-era, the Last World, in which the heavenly and earthly realms are no longer separate but have become fully unified. I must insist that in my worldview there is only one world, and it is this world, the world that our ordinary language gives us. And this world is in no sense merely a preliminary, probationary world in which we are tested and trained to get ourselves ready for our true and final home after this life in the World Above. If for a moment I were to al-low such thoughts to enter, my whole philosophy of life would begin to be corrupted by dualism and by ulteriority. I'd cease to be solar: I'd stop giving 100 percent to this life now, and start instead to hope for vindication, compensation, reward hereafter. And so I would fall prey to the negative emotions again. I'd start looking sideways at people who seem to be doing better than I am, and resenting their relative good fortune. Nietzsche has well described the divided psychology that results: I may appear out-wardly unctuous, smiling and harmless, but underneath there is a great deal of rancour and desire for revenge upon my enemies.

Nietzsche finds this religious psychology especially in the Gospel of John. I prefer to avoid that distracting suggestion, and instead point to wartime heroines such as Nurse Edith Cavell and Etty Hillesum, who tried to live without hatred even in the most extreme and terrifying circumstances. They understood that because the external world is projected out from within our own hearts, and tends to reflect our own feeling for good or ill, dualism and ambivalent feeling in one area quickly spreads to others. Short-term and long-term, this life and the next,

appearance and reality, superficial unction and deep vindictive-
ness, we the good people and they the evil empire, the enemies
of God, the elect and the reprobate, the sheep and the goats, in-
siders and outsiders—repeatedly, we divide up the self, the world
and time into two asymmetrical groups or zones or periods. The
one with which we identify ourselves and perhaps our audience
is now doing a bit less well than it deserves, and the other, from
which we distance ourselves, is heading for a nasty shock. So it
is that people's desire to see justice done is very often driven by
hatred and a desire for revenge, and *philadelphia* (brotherly love)
is often cemented by a shared xenophobia (dislike of outsiders).

Against that whole complex of ideas, I want to insist that in
order to make the world a better place, we must not call for
divine intervention in support of our cause; we must get all the
dualistic thinking, the ressentiment, the ill-feeling, out of our
own hearts. We'll never know anything but this. There is only
this world. To make it a better place we need to live without
the value-contrasts that divide manifest from latent, our own
people from the heathen Others, and short-term from long-term
well-being. We need to live as completely without oppositional,
ambivalent thinking and feeling as we can be, even to the point
of not hating our bitterest enemies and critics, and not even
dreaming of seeing them get their comeuppance.

So no reward, definitely no reward. It is possible to have joy
in life even while one is under sentence of death. Solar living is
'eternal life' in that it makes possible an indestructible happiness
here and now. We cannot and may not ask for more. If we can
do solar living, we need nothing more.

Note, finally, that on my view rewards are systematically pre-
cluded. I am nothing but a cluster of interpretations of my own
process of self-expenditure. The self is not preserved 'unto everlasting life': in solar living it simply, joyfully, and wholly expends
itself. When it is gone—in death, there is nothing of it left to
reward.

Death cannot be cheated, and I would not even try. For example, I have no idea of whether anyone in the future will ever read carefully what I have written, and I don't care. I can't care. I'm glad enough to have tried to be solar, and to have been able to say what I have had to say. That is all.[25]

16

Morality
and Mortality

Perhaps the main event that should be shaping today's religious thought is the widespread abandonment of belief in any personal life after death. After the First World War, the belief still meant much to many people; but since the 1960s, with the decline of tradition, it has faded. More generally, we have also seen the end of the old communal hopes, the eschatologies that used to promise us all a better world in the future, whether here below or in heaven after death. We often hear ordinary people raising some question about what is to be done, or what may happen 'when I'm gone', but they do not suggest anything about 'where I'll be'. That is a topic about which there is no longer anything to say. Increasingly, we see ourselves as woven into nature, and the disappearance of a once-fervent public interest in spiritualism and 'psychical research' together indicate that life after death has ceased to be a live issue. When did you last hear serious talk about ghosts? Not for decades.

Interestingly, Philip Larkin is one of many writers who suggest that religion was first 'created to pretend we never die'—with the further implication that if life after death is no longer a live issue, then religion as a whole is no longer a live issue. Several critics have suggested that a religious book, a first-hand religious book, is no longer a serious literary possibility. Why? Presumably because religion is the orientation of life towards a supernatural world: but there is no such world. If you want to smuggle religion into the pages of a leading literary journal, you can do so only by writing an historical-critical work about a person who has undoubted literary standing, and had the good fortune to live in an age when religion was still a serious subject. Possible examples are Rowan Williams' book about Dostoyevsky, and John Drury's about George Herbert. These excellent works are religious writing at one remove, reminding me of the remark of one of my own commissioning editors: 'In Britain many people write books about theology, but I rarely encounter a book of theology'.

It has all slipped into the past tense now. Serious religion is a dead subject. There is no space left for it on most people's mental map.

It is admittedly true that people still try to cheat death in a surprising variety of ways. They may think of downloading their minds into computers, and then of becoming immortal within the virtual worlds of the far future. There has been talk of living on within the divine memory, as the still-lamented Kathleen Ferrier and Jacqueline du Pré live on in their recordings, and Edward Elgar lives on thrice when his person is filmed conducting, giving us his own interpretation of his own music. (Several earlier composers cut pianola recordings of their own music, too.) But whatever kind of monument or recording or personal art-product one may construct, everyone understands that it does not and cannot really 'cheat death'. We can all guess that William Shakespeare never knew, and therefore never derived any consolation from, the fact that he was going to become 'Shakespeare', and that although Picasso probably knew perfectly well that he was himself one of the most spectacularly-gifted of all human beings, it was of no comfort at all when in his very last works the nonagenarian Picasso confronted his own death. It was just as dark and fearsome a prospect for him as it is for everyone else.

Death cannot be cheated, then. What is the effect upon religion? Our perspective is drastically shortened. Today is the best day I have left to me. In our later years, there's no need or time for ulteriority, long-term planning or saving. I should begin solar living, an all-out, generous affirmation of life, today. It is indeed rational to be extraverted, to think of others, to put one's own affairs in order and to be as generous as I can to anyone around me who needs help. But the central policy is to commit oneself into life, and to treat all value henceforth as intrinsic. If I can carry this policy all the way through, and surrender myself completely into my own transience, 'dying daily'—then death disappears, and there is only immortal love, eternal life in a standing Now.

Experimentally, I can only report in an autobiographical way a few occasions when I have been suddenly struck by an overwhelming *Lebensgefühl*. When I was young, it might come almost anywhere, as once at the bus stop outside the R. C. Cathedral in Salford, Lancashire. Otherwise, it has been mainly outdoors, linked with sunlight and with insects and birds.

So far as religion is concerned, the end of belief in any personal life after death thus seems to have the effect of precipitating us into life now, in the present moment. It immerses us into a form of extravertive visual mysticism: we are lost in love for the world, for the shimmering flux of phenomena, and for all life.

So far, so familiar, you may think. But now suppose we ask a parallel series of questions about morality. When we lose belief in any personal life after death, what happens to ethics—to our sense of enduring moral responsibility, to values, to the moral worth of a large project, and to our love for the dead?

Before we can answer this question, two preliminary points need to be made. The first is that because in my philosophy language is only human, and our knowledge is only human; and because we cannot avoid a certain anthropocentrism, for we can never stand wholly outside ourselves—because of these things, for me ethics is only human. We don't know, for the meanwhile at least, of any non-human moral agent or repository of values. In our everyday speech, people nowadays frequently refer to 'human values', but we no longer hear much about 'absolute values', supposedly subsisting somewhere outside the human realm and independent of us. Kant, with his famously a priori approach to morals, produced a formal theory which would be applicable to any and every kind of rational moral agent that there might be. For him, ethics was not only for humans. But for me it is.

And that brings me to my second point. In the late modern period, when the mass media, and now many new information technologies, have immersed us in a torrent of daily communication, and we have become highly aware of rapid cultural change, we have to see our moral institutions, values and practices as being always culturally embedded. Like it or not, I here find myself seeing the point of Hegel's treatment of ethics. We have to give up all attempts to locate the truth of our moral beliefs in a timeless realm outside history. On the contrary, with our long adult lives nowadays, we have all had the experience of undergoing considerable change in our own moral convictions. It seems that morality is cultural, and has a human history.

These two points—that we cannot nowadays do other than see morality as human, and as being always embedded in contemporary culture and history—lead us to a third thesis, namely that all forms of law-morality are now inappropriate. Before the rise of science, the cosmos was modelled on the state. It was governed by a wise and benevolent Providence, who had built into it a system of natural moral laws binding upon moral creatures such as ourselves. When after Newton mathematical physics triumphed, it became harder to see the 'natural moral law' as being built into the way the world works. Nature had come to be modelled purely mathematically. Kant then attempted to replace natural law with a rational moral law worked out purely a priori. It consisted in a system of categorically-binding imperative principles that we can think of as binding everyone equally, and as obliging each of us to treat each other always as an end and never merely as a means.

Kant's theory sets up the moral community as a network of subjects, each of whom has the same rights and duties vis-à-vis all the others. The whole system is very formalistic and masculinist, opposing duty to inclination. The good life is a life of doing one's duty just for duty's sake, and Kant so separates morality from our temporal life of feeling that he declares moral action to be timeless. But he thinks we must believe that we can make moral progress, and therefore that we should maintain a minimal 'postulate of immortality' in which to complete our strenuous task of self-improvement.

Today, all forms of law-ethic—the natural moral law, God's revealed Ten Commandments, Kant's categorical imperative—are fast fading. The whole vocabulary of law and obedience, duty and conscience, unchanging absolutes, and the rest is falling into disuse. It is too cerebral, and it leaves too much out. It tells us nothing at all about what a truly morally good person of today might be like, nor about what qualities of character we should most profoundly respect and admire. In our world we who live after Darwin and Freud have become highly aware of our own animal nature, and of our own immersion in a life of flowing feelings—both expressions of feeling and feeling-responses. We can't easily even imagine a moral theory that completely separates morality from feeling.

More conclusively still, all law-moralities regard themselves as preparatory and disciplinary, being laid down to govern a period when we are like schoolchildren being trained in the self-discipline we'll need later on, when we leave our schooldays behind and venture forth into the openness and freedom of adult life. Today, however, we are already in the last world we'll ever know. Asceticism, living under rule in preparation for a bigger and better life hereafter, is obviously a waste of time, and it is not surprising that the old religious orders of monks and nuns are now shrinking so quickly. I'd do better, and we'd all do better, simply to make the most of life while we have it.

In this situation, it is easy to understand the modern popularity of an Aristotelean style of virtue-ethics. In a post-metaphysical society, people are most easily recognized and identified as individuals by their habits, and a virtue is a continuing habitual disposition to behave in such-and-such an observable way. I would find it very hard to recognise you via the laws you are obeying, or even to know what they are, unless you take the time to spell them out to me. But it is very easy for your friends to recognize a particular habitual pattern in your behaviour as identifying you as virtuous (or perhaps not, as the case may be). We say, 'By that, I'd know him anywhere', 'That's him all over!', 'I'd expect no less from him', and so on.

In a rapidly-changing world, we are often worried about how it is that we are able to recognize the continuing personal identity of ourselves and our friends. And we are also often concerned about how we see what may be very varied bits of human behaviour as falling under general descriptions and rules, and therefore counting as expressions of a person's moral character, and as exemplifying some particular virtue or vice. Aristotelian virtue ethics, used in our talk about our friends and our daily interaction with them, does very well in explaining all this. I don't need to be able to recognize law-breaking and sin or guilt in other people, but I do need to be able to recognize moral qualities in the patterns of 'typical' observable behaviour through which I identify them as my friends.

One further comment on our present theme of morality and mortality. Nietzsche and some others of his period thought we should try to leave behind us a life that is like a completed work of art. But because death can come at any time, I can never be sure of living to complete any large-scale work upon which I am engaged. Does it not follow that in my later years I should not agree to embark on any large-scale project, for fear that I will leave it unfinished?

I don't agree. In fact we are touchingly reminded of our own contingency when a gifted young person dies prematurely. Often, we are strongly moved to love, as everyone is by the death of John Keats, or by the recorded voice of Kathleen Ferrier. Something sadly cut short is not thereby ruined aesthetically, not at all. It is part of life's poignant bitter-bittersweetness that there are many such cases.

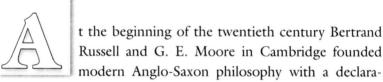

17

Philosophy of Life as First Philosophy

At the beginning of the twentieth century Bertrand Russell and G. E. Moore in Cambridge founded modern Anglo-Saxon philosophy with a declaration of war against all forms of edifying, inspirational, preachy, human philosophy. No longer would philosophy be a pallid, uplifting replacement for religion. Instead, it was going to start with philosophical logic, philosophy of mathematics, and theory of knowledge. Indeed, it would largely limit itself to that syllabus. Its principal patron saint was David Hume, and it became very tough, combative and masculinist. In a few decades it had captured the majority of university teaching posts in philosophy across the English-speaking world, and reached its high point of prestige and influence at Oxford during the third quarter of the twentieth century.

The Oxford philosophers soon earned a reputation for elitism. They looked down their noses at able contemporaries such as K. R. Popper and Ernest Gellner, whose only fault was that they had come originally from Central Europe, and now worked in London. The Oxford philosophers seemed to regard themselves as Platonic philosopher-rulers whose special gifts and training had entitled them to speak as if from a superior viewpoint. They could think, argue and write more clearly than lesser mortals.

Meanwhile, however, the cultural setting of modern philosophy was changing. Higher education was being rapidly expanded, democratized, and even feminized. In ordinary language a person's 'philosophy' is still recognizably a version of human philosophy: it is in effect a small group of practical principles that together add up to a general policy for living. In the lecture rooms, the older male analytic philosophers found themselves confronting an audience half female, often oriented towards human philosophy, and interested in recent French thinkers. The one modern, and at least adoptively British, philosopher whose ideas might be of interest to this new, more democratic audience was Ludwig Wittgenstein, who was unfortunately not an Oxford man. But some very good people at Oxford (Pears, Baker, Hacker) wrote excellent books about Wittgenstein in which they did their level best to turn him into a highly-respectable Oxford philosopher.

Against this well-known background, a lesser mortal from another place may perhaps be allowed to admire their work. The sheer violence and vastness of the twentieth century's cultural explosion blew up all 'foundations' and all would-be totalizing systems of thought, whether metaphysical or political or religious. The celebrated Gödel's theorem seemed to prove that strict logical totalization was itself an impossible, unrealizable ideal. Even natural science, despite its spectacular progress, was not immune to great theoretical upheavals which left one wondering how it could ever have been received and understood dogmatically. In an increasingly turbulent, plural and globalized world, where could we locate our common ground: where was it reasonable for us to feel most at home and secure? It is not surprising that many people, thinking of Socrates in the market place, should reply: if in a bewildered age we want to find our own best home ground, we should begin with ordinary language and try to understand what it is, and how it is used in daily life to further the purposes of life. Think of a schoolteacher, teaching

French. The teacher gets the pupils to act out the simple roles and life-situations in which we make a purchase, order a meal, buy a ticket and so on. As we learn the skill of playing these little language-games we are beginning to feel more comfortable. We begin to understand what ordinary language is, and how it works. We are on language's own home ground. This is where we all began, and it is the place to which we should return if we are trying to make a new beginning.

More recently, enthusiasm for Wittgenstein's method and outlook has waned. Much of his ground is now covered with greater technical precision and sophistication by modern linguistics—yet another example of science taking over, and managing more professionally, a territory that formerly belonged to philosophy. It may be retorted that 'there is always a remainder' which linguistics 'leaves unthought'. There is some truth in that, and Derrida's philosophy is the best attempt yet to think, and to articulate clearly, that unthought remainder.

Meanwhile I stick with the view that when the present bonfire of all the faiths and philosophies has died down, we are still likely to find ourselves saying that our best way of beginning the task of reconstruction is by an attempt to understand ordinariness, ordinary language and ordinary life. Ordinary life is always presupposed, and will always be the matrix within which all our more specialized activities are carried on.

I'll add a little more: life is not only the buzz of activity that we create by our own jostling, our attempts to attract attention, and our competing initiatives and interpretations; life is also something bigger than ourselves, into which we enter. It is a flowing stream of often-ambivalent feelings that pours out of us into public expression and is there read as a stream of symbolic meaning. Somehow, in us humans, outpouring feeling turns into discourse, consecutive thought. At what point? I'm unsure. Indeed, all the frontiers in this area, between nature and culture, between material culture and ideal culture, between language and its Other, and so forth are nowadays constantly shifting and disputed.

We are living in an age in which we must attempt to democratize high culture. We want to leave behind us the idea that 'the top'—the highest and most thrilling area of cultural life, the place of creation, destruction and recreation—can be accessed only by a very small and specially-trained élite. Indeed, I have already claimed elsewhere that close examination shows ordinary language to be philosophically much subtler than you might expect.

So much for my suggestion that in our future work of reconstruction, we should see the philosophy of life as first philosophy. It's democratic: it is everywhere and is always presupposed. It is practical: it is about values, and about how we should live by our own delicately-evaluative life of feeling, as it comes out into symbolic expression, and as we thereby make each of us our own contribution to the building and rebuilding of the common world.

Along these lines we can look back now to the pessimism of the later Heidegger during the twenty years or so after 1945. After one-and-a-half centuries of world leadership in culture— and especially in philosophy and music—Germany during the Hitler years had suffered perhaps the worst and most utterly demoralizing disaster that any nation has ever suffered. Even today, Germans still find it difficult to talk about their years of collective moral insanity—and Heidegger knew well enough that he personally had not exactly shone: indeed, given who he was, his own record was part of that disaster. Western culture's centuries of world dominance were at an end, and Europe stared nihilism in the face. It waited in the darkness, hoping for a new dawn, one day. Heidegger thought that as we waited we should attempt to return into the pre-Socratic origins of our tradition, and try to prepare ourselves for a new relation to Being.

Trying to respond to Heidegger's suggestion, I have rewritten Being as Be-ing, by way of reminding myself of the temporality of all being; and then have rewritten Be-ing as life, by way of bringing out what it is. It is a continuously outpouring stream of highly-sensitive biological feelings that, as they come out into expression, get coded into signs, and so became part of the ceaseless noisy conversation of humanity which builds and rebuilds our common world.

This connects us again with our main theme in this book, the priority of ethics in regenerative religious thought. Marxism pointed out that philosophy from Plato to Kant had usually begun by describing and vindicating presently-established reality, and then it advised us to conform ourselves to its law. The theologians had done the same. They had borrowed from philosophy a picture of reality as a graded hierarchy of degrees of power, perfection and goodness. The cosmos was an absolute monarchy, it was the mother and father of all absolute monarchies, and you had better conform yourself to the will of God the Supreme Being. You should 'worship the King / all-glorious Above, / O gratefully sing / his power and his love'; because if you displeased him at all you would incur his infinite wrath. You'd fry for all eternity, deservedly. That was 'realist' religion, being prudent. But Heidegger in his last years lived in a time of fearsome destruction. For the Germans, present reality had been comprehensively wiped out, rather as, for us who live half-a-century later, present reality is frail and (unless we change our own behaviour greatly) could be heading for self-destruction.

In a time of imminent or actual destruction, how should we live? Not by looking to present reality to shape our lives, but by looking to a vision of how the ordinary life-world could and should be in future, and then beginning gradually to make it come true. Most religions may eventually become conservative and traditionalist, but they all began as innovations. A visionary founder and teacher had a dream about what human life might possibly become, and his early followers tried to codify, to propagate, and to live the Dream. Their faith was anticipatory, living the Dream in advance of its arrival.

The case of Jesus is particularly striking. He lived at a time of great pressure, when eschatological expectation was strong. For many, this meant the coming of the 'kingdom of God' on earth. Jesus preaches that the kingdom of God is indeed coming, and by way of supporting evidence we are given a summary of his activities. This is apparently derived from Q, and is found in Matthew 11:2–6 and Luke 7:18–23. It is mainly a list of his humanitarian actions, which themselves foreshadow the new world that they are bringing in. Even more striking is the content of Jesus' teaching. The parables and sayings do not tell us about goings on in the supernatural world. No, not at all; Jesus simply presents us with scenes from everyday life. They illustrate an essentially ethical approach to religious truth. If we want to see the better human life-world we say we long for, we need to learn that our own hearts are too often full of ressentiment—envy, meanness of spirit, and desire for revenge. The better world will have come when we have learnt to live generously, to live always by love and never by ressentiment, actively forgiving and actively seeking reconciliation.

In this we see how philosophy and theology could perhaps draw closer together again after having been separated in the West for centuries. They can both base themselves on the best things we have left to us in these difficult times. The primacy of ethics, democratic ordinariness, humanitarianism and freely-flowing feeling: the philosophy of life.

Philosophy of Life as Fundamental Theology

I t should be no surprise, at this stage in the argument, to learn that I propose to ground not only philosophy, but also theology, in the world of ordinary human life. We have after all said that we need to go back to a period before philosophy and religious thought became separated from each other. But there is a great deal more yet to be said about the remarkable history of religious truth in our own tradition. David Friedrich Strauss observes that 'the best criticism of doctrine is the history of doctrine', and he is clearly right.

For theological reasons, we are strongly attached to a highly-monarchical view of religious truth, so much so that Americans I have quizzed about it are puzzled to explain how they combine fervent attachment to liberal democracy here on earth with their equally fervent belief in absolute monarchy at the cosmic level. The Roman Catholic Church in particular trades upon that belief in absolute monarchy: One Church, one papacy, One Faith, One Lord—*semper eadem*, always the same. So popular is the idea that people are easily persuaded that the mediaeval Latin Church was already 'Roman Catholic', and even that the early church too was ruled from Rome by a line of successors of St Peter. We forget that according to the New Testament itself several other churches—that of Syria, for example—are older than the Roman church. And we forget that from the Eastern Christian point of view the Western Patriarch, he of Rome, was only one of five or more great Patriarchs. When Constantine moved his capital to Constantinople, the Ecumenical Patriarch of Constantinople became a bigger figure than the Western Patriarch, who ruled only a relatively poor and remote end of the Mediterranean world. The serious money was in 'the gorgeous East'.

There was no pope in those days. When the Constantinian church found itself troubled with an acute doctrinal disagreement, and urgently needed a major conference to reach and enforce unity, the leading bishops called upon, not the bishop of Rome, but the emperor to convoke it. Which he did. Thus the first great council of the undivided Church, that of Nicea, was called by the emperor and not by the pope, who did not turn up in person; and the standard Christian doctrine of the divinity of Christ was defined in the imperial interest, because in those days the emperor was (iconographically) Christ's earthly counterpart. The Church even came fairly close, at the time of Constantine's funeral, to giving semi-divine status to the emperor.

Early Christianity had certainly not begun with the degree of doctrinal unity that the emperors desired to see. The striking miscellany of writings that came to be called the New Testament is a strange mixture of different interpretations of Jesus and his legacy, selected from an even wider diversity of apocryphal writings. The Church was aware of its own need for an agreed apostolic faith, if it was to keep its identity at all. Accordingly, it developed the idea that all eleven (or twelve) apostles were personal witnesses to the resurrection of Jesus, and all of them had been commissioned by him to teach all humanity a short formula which had eventually developed into your own local baptismal creed.

Scattered over the world, each apostle became (or so it was claimed) the first bishop of an Apostolic See, passing his own oral testimony on to his successors in office. Thus, if you had doubts, you should consult the nearest occupant of an Apostolic See, and through him you could tap into an oral tradition that went directly back to the mouth of the Risen Lord himself.

Such was the principal early notion of religious truth and how to locate it accurately. If you 'wanted it in writing', then the Church during the first few centuries gradually developed a canonical body of scriptures, and at the major councils and synods a body of doctrinal definitions and disciplinary rulings. In due course there developed the notion of an original orthodoxy ('the myth of the normative origin'), Christianity's pure and primitive 'essence', the 'deposit of faith' revealed to the first followers of Jesus and sailing on unchanged down the centuries, resisting the assaults of heretics on the right hand and on the left. From this notion of a divinely-protected tradition of orthodoxy stem the later beliefs in the indefectibility and even infallibility of the Church.

But in fact, of course, it was not like that at all. The notions of revealed religious truth, of the teaching office of the bishops, of orthodoxy and heresy and so on developed only slowly through a complex and often very untidy human history. Some at least of the 'heretics', such as Marcion and Arius, were arguably more nearly in the right than their 'orthodox' opponents. It did not help them.

It also needs to be said that 'orthodoxy' was never as tidy and complete as it was claimed to be. The totality that people call 'Christianity' is in many respects painfully fissured. For example, the doctrine of the saving work of Christ was never defined. Ask yourself, then, what it is that supposedly 'saves' us humans and unites us with God? Is it the incarnation of God in Christ, by which the Incarnate Lord is 'consubstantial' both with God the Father and with us humans; or is it the saving work of Christ, through which Jesus has borne the penalty for our sins? The Eastern Orthodox will tend to say the former, and the Reformed will tend to say the latter—opening a painful fissure.

On a wider front, serious apologetics, systematizing and explaining the basic doctrines of faith, and carefully setting out and
debating the evidence and arguments for and against their truth,
did not really exist at all until the Enlightenment. The *Contra
Celsum* of Origen is one of the very few creditable exceptions to
the general rule. Otherwise, before printing, books were very
few and very expensive. It was customary to treat all books, and
not only the scriptures, as authoritative. Traditionalism keeps
everything, thinking it a sin to discard anything. Accordingly,
even the best systematic theologians, such as Augustine of Hippo
and John of Damascus, simply heaped together everything that
reached them, and wove or narrated it all into a big, loose, untidy synthesis. Some of them were quite good philosophers, but
otherwise it has to be said that by our modern intellectual standards they had no method at all, because they could not coun-
tenance the idea of critically sifting the evidence and discarding
material that did not stand up. On the contrary, Holy Tradition
was a sacred totality, and you could not thin it out. It was a duty
to be uncritical. Their reading of texts was so poor that it is not
easy to find any Christian writers before the Enlightenment who
have looked closely at the language used by the Jesus of St John's
Gospel, and have seen that his vocabulary and his thought are
extraordinarily different from the Jesus of the first three gospels.

Confirming the same point, Tatian's Diatessaron of ca. 150 CE
was a single continuous gospel compiled by cutting and pasting
all four canonical gospels together. This compilation simply loses
all the significant differences between the canonical gospels, but
it was so popular that in Syria it was long used in the liturgy instead of the four gospels. People actually preferred it.

Another example: a 'legend' is an edifying passage from the
Lives of the Saints, to be read aloud during mealtimes in a house
of religion. Even in those days, the lives of the saints were so
preposterous, and so full of absurd pious fictions, that they became a byword.

And a final example: in those days, it was accepted as being normally your duty that you should go along with and accept the beliefs, and indeed the whole religious system, that was accepted as authoritative in your own society. Consent was normally correct, and dissent was prima facie sinful and wrong.

All of which is sufficient to indicate that by our modern critical standards, the Christianity of the period up to about 1600 cannot sensibly be described as 'true' or 'false'. It had no standards. It was pre-critical. It was simply an untidy, accumulated cultural tradition, an entity like a language, or a civilization; but it knew nothing of our modern intellectual standards, and never expected to be required to meet them. It had not yet even invented our ideas of research, and of a large, organized, tested body of knowledge. By our standards, they had some quite good philosophy and some very good ethics. They had highly-developed craft skills in such areas as architecture, sculpture, ship-building, metal working and so on. But their medicine, their theorizing of the natural world around them, and their historical knowledge were almost non-existent.

Against this background we can understand how weak were such apologetic arguments as they did in fact produce. Thus in the flush of satisfaction caused by the Church's sudden coming into imperial favour in the early fourth century, Eusebius of Caesarea produces two great 'evidences' of the truth of Christianity. They are, first, the *praeparatio evangelica,* the providential preparation of the pagan world to receive the gospel of Christ; and second, the speed with which early Christian faith had spread around the Mediterranean. After Eusebius, these two feeble claims were copied from writer to writer for over a millennium without, I think, any Christian noticing that a Muslim apologist might use both of them with much more justification. Islamic civilization spread and matured far more quickly than that. Take a look at the Dome of the Rock, built around AH 68–70, that is, very soon after the Prophet's death, and ask yourself how long it took for

Christian architecture to reach that remarkable level. Perhaps the best comparison would be with Justinian's churches at Ravenna in north Italy, built five centuries after Jesus' death.

In those pre-critical times then, people got by, as they always had got by, on a mixture of craft-skills, rules of thumb, custom, tradition and personal experience—but hardly any critically tested and purged knowledge at all. Christianity had never been asked to justify itself by the sort of standards that were first introduced by Descartes (*Discourse on Method*, 1637), and were then presented to it in the form of a direct challenge by the Deists. At Cambridge, some theologians like Whiston asked themselves: 'On the new map of the cosmos drawn by Newton, where are we to locate heaven? And indeed, hell?'—and they realized that this was an entirely new sort of problem, to which there was no easy answer.

For the first time in Christian history, it was necessary for Christian writers to explain themselves to an audience that found bewildering lines like 'He ascended into heaven'. How is such language to be interpreted and justified? Confronted now with the need to present Christian teachings in a more nearly rational and intellectually defensible form, theologians made a broad distinction between rational or natural theology, and revealed theology.

Rational theology consisted of those religious doctrines which had been quite widely held by the philosophers in late antiquity: the existence, power and goodness of a (realist, metaphysical) God, who was the Supreme Being; the existence and immortality of the human rational soul, made in God's image; God's requirement of human worship and service; the living of a good life at the best part of such service; and the Last Judgement at the end of history, at which the final destinies they merit will be allocated to each and every human being.

So much for the traditional rational theology. It was finally wiped out intellectually by Hume and Kant, and since the 'atheism controversy' at Jena in 1799/1800 there has been no serious likelihood that it will ever be reinstated amongst philosophers.[26]

Next, eighteenth-century apologetics had a transitional passage about humanity's failure to live up to its high status and promised destiny. The human world has now fallen into a corrupt and ruinous state, and is desperately in need of redemption. So bad have things become that only God is powerful, wise and benevolent enough to accomplish man's redemption—his aim being to restock heaven, where the fall and banishment of Lucifer and the rebel angels had left numbers depleted. Then there follows a full exposition of biblical theology and of the two great covenants, the law of Moses and the gospel of Jesus Christ.

The Catholic version of this revealed theology worked under the general rubric: 'The Church to teach, and the Bible to prove.' The Reformed Protestant version said simply that 'the inward testimony of the Holy Spirit' makes the whole truth of the plan of salvation evident to the diligent and faithful Christian student of the Bible.

All this was made obsolete by the rise during the eighteenth century of modern biblical criticism at the German universities, the single best and most illuminating story being that of the life and work of D. F. Strauss.[27] By the later nineteenth century word had gone round: most of the literate and educated middle classes, and a number of theologians with them, now knew that Latin Christian Theology is not in fact true by modern (that is, critical) standards.

The problem was partly solved by making three moves. The middle-class laity went over more-or-less openly (usually, less) to cultural Christianity. They continued to accept the ethics which amongst us is now described as 'humanitarian', while they in effect put all the supernatural doctrine on the back burner, treating it as well-loved but now obsolete cultural clothing in which the ethics had traditionally been dressed up, and which they sincerely wish to keep at hand for reasons of cultural continuity. Fifty years ago the cultural Christians included many artists like Auden and Britten, who were well content to be seen by the public as Christians. But today they also include many open unbelievers, such as Richard Dawkins, Philip Pullman and Roger Scruton, as well as the liberal bishops and most of the leading theologians.

The second move, made especially by these same theologians, was and is the retreat into history. They limit themselves to historical criticism of and scholarly familiarity with, the Christian scriptures, the history of theology, church history and so on. In effect, they say, 'This is what Christianity was, and as for the question of exactly how much of it can be believed by us today, you must answer that for yourself. For my part, I'm not coming out publicly; not ever.'

The third move, then, behind this carefully-maintained screen, is to do as much putting on the back burner, repositioning, and reshuffling as can be done without ever 'coming out'. The highest rewards are given to those theologians who, by being both scholarly and personally 'reserved', most successfully prolong modern Christianity's intellectual agony. Popular nostalgia for the old religion that we have now lost is so great that even the shell of it that remains is greatly loved. In general, people will cling to an orthodoxy that they no longer believe in, rather than embrace a rational revision of it that is unfamiliar and unloved.

A very curious, easy-to-miss corollary of all this is that a modern bishop who does not attempt any sort of modern intellectual defence of his beliefs, but simply accepts them from tradition and functions with them, may indeed look to us like a mere 'cultural Christian'; but in reality his intellectual position is the position that everybody was in before the seventeenth century! By modern standards, he doesn't believe any more than, say, Richard Dawkins or Philip Pullman do; but by historical standards, which were very, very low, he is orthodox.

The paradox is amusing. Most of the laity and at least half of the clergy are nowadays merely cultural Christians. On substantive issues, they do not really disagree with Philip Pullman. But they are sincere. They use the words, accepting them from tradition, and going along with all that the other believers do. So that should be enough. Shouldn't it? The historic Church never supposed that one day people might expect of believers the sort of super-rational and super-critical standards that are required of a modern scientific researcher, testing a new medicine.

I suspect that modern media people understand the situation. They know, church people know, we all of us know, that by the standards of modern critical rationality Christianity is not strictly true. But nor does anybody wish to ban the school nativity play on the grounds that by modern standards of rationality it is well-known to be just a pious fiction, a bit of midrash devised to show the fulfilment of prophecy in the birth of Jesus. So the media are content to set aside all questions of metaphysics and supernatural belief, and instead simply classify the believers and their fellow-travellers politically. There are the conservative traditionalists, and standing close to them there are the (unbelieving) cultural Christians, who love the old liturgy, the old translation and the old ways generally; and there are the liberals, who think we might do a bit better if we were to modernize some of those old ways. On this basis, the media people can report all the factional fighting, the posturing and the play-acting that goes on. None of it is serious, because serious modern belief is not, and has never been possible. Modern belief is always in some measure ironical, because it also half-admits that it is unavoidably tainted by unbelief. The old religion could not prepare us for the unprecedented cultural situation in which we now find ourselves.

The major exceptions to this generalization are the early Methodists and Evangelicals, including the post-Evangelical John Henry Newman.[28] These people responded to the rise of experimental natural science by maintaining that the realistic, objective Truth of Christian supernatural beliefs could be verified in the believer's personal subjective experience, and proved to the general public by an otherwise-inexplicable conversion of life. The Evangelicals believed that their appeal to experience gave them the realist credentials that they craved. It was a thoroughly bad argument, for it goes in a circle: first my beliefs shape my experience, and then I start claiming that my experience confirms the truth of my beliefs! So this whole system of thought is quite wrong, but it played a large part in religious history and is unfortunately not dead even yet.

Thus we return to the plight of religious thought at top level today. It is not serious, and today even the most senior church leaders know that it is all sadly collapsing. The intellectual breakdown of Catholic philosophy and of supernatural doctrine is at least a factor in the moral collapse of the clergy, not least in the Roman church. We are not meeting top standards, either intellectually or morally. Our church controversies are play-acting. We are not serious, and in our hearts we know it. I for one feel that it is necessary to attempt a fresh start if anything of religion in general, and Christianity in particular, is to be preserved.

What do we have left to us? Only two things: the figure of Jesus, who is not to blame for the errors of the Christian Church and who still attracts well-nigh universal respect, and the infinitely-precious, still-vigorous tradition of humanitarian ethics that derives ultimately from his teaching.

Another legacy item needs to be noted. There are no longer two distinct worlds, earth and heaven, the natural and the supernatural. As Church-Christianity completes its historic task, the two worlds come together and fuse into just one world, the world of everyday human life.

This last observation helps us to fulfil the requirement of those who say that we need to go back to the days in antiquity before religion and philosophy became separated. I take philosophy back to human philosophy, and in particular the philosophy of ordinary human life in the life-world, to which the current use of ordinary language gives us the key; and I take religious thought back to its origins in a period (the Palaeolithic) before the earthly and heavenly worlds had fully drawn apart from each other. In those days the religious imagination shaped the way people saw the natural world.

My version of naturalism says: 'There is only one world, and it is the world which ordinary language gives us, the ordinary human life-world. But because in the modern era the old sacred world has been brought down into this world (the 'sacralization of life'), it is possible to think of living the ethics of Jesus in this present age; and because it is we ourselves who by our buzzing activity largely generate the world of our life, it is we ourselves who—by the way we live—can make it all come true.'

With which we now bring to an end the curious history of religious truth in our religious and cultural tradition. It does not have much of past, but we can give it a better future, if we will but try.[29]

Notes

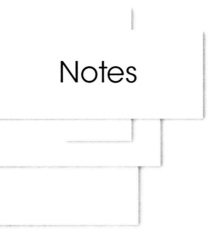

1. Nelson Mandela, *Long Walk to Freedom* (London: Little, Brown and Company, 1994). This is a political autobiography, and not a spiritual or intellectual one, so that there is not as much detail about the religious and moral influences that shaped Mandela's thinking as one might wish to have. He went to a Methodist mission school, and remained an avowed Methodist, but later on gets to know Anglicans such as Huddleston and Tutu.

2. In the Oxford World's Classics series, Tolstoy's principal religious writings are published under the following titles: *A Confession, The Gospel in Brief,* and *What I Believe* (vol. 229); *What Then Must We Do?* (vol. 281); and *The Kingdom of God* and *Peace Essays* (vol. 445). Elsewhere, they may occasionally be found with different titles, but I have to confess that their popularity was part of an early-twentieth-century world which is now completely forgotten.

3. There are presently signs, especially in the United States, of a revival of interest in Marcion. Jason BeDuhn recently published the first English reconstruction of Marcion's edition of the New Testament, *The First New Testament* (Polebridge, 2013).

4. The literature on Schweitzer and his influence on New Testament studies is very large and still growing. See, in particular, the editorial material in Albert Schweitzer, *The Quest of the Historical Jesus,* first complete ed., ed. John Bowden (London: SCM Press, 2000).

5. Friedrich Nietzsche, *The Will to Power,* trans. Walker Kaufmann and R. J. Hollingdale (New York: Vintage Books, Random House, 1968), 7.

6. *The Last Testament* (London: SCM Press, 2012), 67f.

7. *The Five Gospels: The Search for the Authentic Words of Jesus,* new translation and commentary by Robert W. Funk, Roy W. Hoover, and the Jesus Seminar (New York: Scribner, for Polebridge Press, 1996).

8. I should remark here that the word 'humanitarian' has itself a curiously mixed history. It was first used in a doctrinal context: it denoted an understanding of Jesus Christ that laid almost exclusive stress upon his *human* nature. Then during the 1840s it came to be used in its modern ethical sense, in connection with the new feeling for the sufferings of the poor, and of children in the cheap harsh boarding schools described by Charlotte Brontë and Dickens. But during the next hundred years 'humanitarian' and 'philanthropic' were often used contemptuously by conservative speakers. It was only as recently as the 1980s, perhaps in connection with Bob Geldof's Band Aid, that the word 'humanitarian' suddenly threw off its critics and came into everyday use. However, I have not been able to document this remarkable value-shift.

It would also be useful to know something of how humanitarian ethics became so firmly embedded in the work of the various United Nations agencies. Perhaps through the powerful moral influence of Geneva, and French-speaking Switzerland generally? Soon the history of all this needs to be written.

9. For Illingworth, see his book titles, including *Divine Immanence* (1898). He is deplorably bad: I once found him endeavouring to equate the Holy Spirit with electricity!

10. In 1 Chronicles 13:9f., the Ark is being carried on a new cart. The oxen stumble, and a man named Uzza puts out his hand to steady it. God is angry, and strikes Uzza dead.

That the concentrated sacred kills is a common theme in the Hebrew Bible. From there to Stephen Spielberg it is associated with brilliant light.

11. I venture here the suggestion that it is because Muslims have been so careful to retain full-blast philosophical monotheism in the experience of every Muslim every day, that Muslims find it hard to respect, or even to see any place for, secular education, secular knowledge, and the whole secular sphere of life. By contrast, in Jesus and in much of Christian life God has gone out into scattered immanence, allowing more space for the secular. At last, in Jesus' death, God goes right out into his own final dispersal.

12. The door to all these ideas opened for me while I was recovering from brain surgery for a cerebral aneurysm in 1992/93. See the closing pages of *After All* (1994), and also *Solar Ethics* (1995).

13. In this short discussion I refer to Richard Hooker, *The Laws of Ecclesiastical Polity* (1594, 1597), and especially to the invaluable study, F. Paget, *An Introduction to the Fifth Book of Hooker's Treatise*, etc. (1899).

14. It is because Wordsworth did pick up from Coleridge a smattering of the new German Idealist philosophy that so many of his longer and more philosophical poems end by extolling the greatness of the

human mind, and by saying that we 'half-see, half-create' the world of our experience. See for example 'Home at Grasmere', and the conclusion of 'The Prelude' (1805 version). For a while in the first quarter of the nineteenth century it seemed that a new mutation of Christianity was possible; but it did not quite happen.

15. This chapter title points to Kant's own use of the phrase 'moral faith', which of course has contributed to my thinking.

16. The uses of 'life' are studied in my *The New Religion of Life in Everyday Speech* (London: SCM Press, 1999), *Life, Life* (Santa Rosa CA: Polebridge Press, 2003) and other works of that period. I was attempting to describe a new empirical method for pursuing the study of religion.

17. Obstinately pedantic, I use the verb 'to anticipate' in the now almost obsolete 'literal' sense of 'to seize in advance', or 'to enjoy something in advance of one's actual entitlement to it or possession of it'.

18. Note that ordinary language uses the word 'Dream' in the strict Freudian sense of a wish-fulfilment.

19. I am glad to report that *Etty Hillesum: The Complete Works* has now been published, in English translation, in the Netherlands, and under the guidance of the Smelik family, who became the chief guardians of her legacy. One notes with some sadness that—as happened recently with Vincent van Gogh's letters—the standard edition of a major Dutch figure has to appear in English translation in order to be marketable and, indeed, in order to be read.

20. Like Foucault, David Hume had his major breakdown early in life. He went to France to recover, and there wrote his principal work, *A Treatise of Human Nature*. The breakdown was largely caused by his loss of religious faith, as is clearly hinted in many places in his writings. But he made such a full recovery that Christians who visited him on his deathbed, hoping to gloat over him, were disappointed by his equanimity. Many modern Christians, like Betjeman, are haunted all their lives by the fear of death; whereas many modern post-Christians have learnt to love life enough to be entirely cured of the fear of death. As Tolstoy noted, the love of life, if strong enough, is a kind of return of faith.

21. In this brief chapter I try to synthesize ideas about ethics from various dates in my writing. My first essays go back to the early '60s. *The New Christian Ethics* of 1988 had some ideas, but was horribly obscure. *Solar Ethics* (1995) and more recent writings are clearer. They owe a little to Bataille. I was also much struck by Nikos Kazantzakis' observation that there have been 'three great teachers of mankind': the Buddha, Jesus and Nietzsche. Different though they may seem, each of them wanted to live without ressentiment. Very recently, I have been much touched and impressed by Etty Hillesum.

I mention this surprising miscellany of ideas and names for two reasons. First, ethics is in some ways the most important and the hardest branch of philosophy. Secondly, the philosophers and theologians who are generally regarded as canonical writers on ethics are a very disappointing lot. That includes people like Bonhoeffer and Reinhold Niebuhr. I found I had to try to invent some ideas of my own, with a little help from an odd miscellany of guides.

22. The text can be found at *zenit.org/en/articles/ pope-francis-letter-to-the-founder-of-la-repubblica-italian-newspaper*.

23. Better than Arnold? Yes, in spite of the fact that Browning is deplorably over-productive. By the way, my English teacher was W. C. Sellar, coauthor of *1066 and All That*. From him I got my love of Browning.

24. It is a pleasure to recommend C. S. Lewis's excellent old book *The Allegory of Love*, 1936.

25. I first began to latch on to these ideas whilst writing the chapter of *Taking Leave of God* (1980), entitled 'Doctrine and Disinterestedness'. Earlier, in the years when I read a great deal about mysticism, I read the controversies about Pure Love which revolved around the figures of Fénelon and Mme Guyon, and were discussed especially by K. E. Kirk in *The Vision of God* (Bampton Lectures 1928, pub. 1931). Mme Guyon's quietist mysticism was a forerunner of what I have called 'non-realism', especially in its lack of any reward motive.

26. In England, the works of Butler and Paley remained popular throughout the nineteenth century, and were prescribed for ordinands. But they served only to cover the period's intellectual weakness, and its lack of knowledge of modern German philosophy. Victorian piety made a huge effort to convert England by building churches and schools, by establishing religious communities and so on. But it all came to nothing, because intellectually it was a house built on sand.

27. If ever you see George Eliot's early works, her translations of Feuerbach and Strauss, snap them up. They are part of the evidence that the English Victorian Age was not all intellectual darkness. On Strauss there is also a good English study: Horton Harris, *David Friedrich Strauss and His Theology* (Cambridge University Press, 1973).

28. Newman began life as a middle-class London Anglican Evangelical. In *The Grammar of Assent* (1870), he is still using an argument from the phenomena of moral experience for the reality of God. A rather similar Catholic argument from the phenomenology of Catholic experience to the truth of Catholic faith had some influence amongst French Catholics (and also in Poland), a lifetime ago.

29. I end with a brief note of the general hypothesis about Christian origins that I have worked with for the past decade or so. It is a phi-

losopher's hypothesis, and therefore follows the general rule that a naturalistic explanation is always to be preferred.

The original Jesus (ca. 4 BCE to ca. 30 CE) was a secular moral teacher. His 'Dream', as I have called it, was in the tradition of the Hebrew prophets, such as Jeremiah 31:31–34. He announced the coming of the kingdom of God *on earth*. He personally acted out some of the traditional signs of its coming, and urged his followers to begin living its life by anticipation, so as to help to make it all come true. One should become completely open and available to others; one should live according to love, without any ressentiment at all; one should practice solar living, not seeking to escape from temporality, but affirming it. We pass away singing.

The small circle of Jesus' followers was very badly shocked by his violent and ignoble death. As often happens today in such cases, a few of his devoted women followers, including Mary of Magdala, may have had hallucinations in which he seemed to be still alive. Groups of Jesus' followers continued to meet in Jerusalem, where they were led by James the Lord's brother; in Galilee, where they were led by Peter; and perhaps in a few other places, such as, possibly, Syria or Egypt. They preserved some good oral traditions of Jesus' teaching, in units of not more than a short sentence in length.

In the late 40s, tensions over the leadership of the community had begun, the main rivalry being that between Peter and James. Picking up on Mary of Magdala's reported vision, Peter and his allies began to claim that Peter had seen the Lord. Jesus was exalted to heaven, was now the Messiah-designate, and would in due course return in power to complete his work. The claim caught on, and the visions spread—to all the apostles, to five hundred brethren at once, to James, and (last of all) to Paul of Tarsus.

The date is now around the year 50, and the infant religion has suddenly undergone a major change. Jesus' message was ethical and this-worldly. He did not encourage any special veneration of himself. But now the believing community became absorbed in looking towards the supernatural world, to the glorified Jesus, and to purifying themselves as they waited for his return in glory. Meanwhile, Peter and the other apostles were becoming a ruling-class élite within the Church. They had the keys of the kingdom, the power of forgiveness. They controlled doctrine, worship and discipline. It was a completely new religion, and the historical Jesus faded out of it at once. The historical traditions of his teaching and his earthly life were soon extensively revised so that they could be read as endorsing the new faith. Just a whiff of the original, pre-50 Jesus remained; enough to keep alive a minority, dissenting tradition within the Church. Interestingly, it re-emerged briefly in the Franciscan movement of the early thirteenth century, which actually won papal approval. Today a Latin American pope has taken the name of Francis, and has suggested the

possibility that even at this date there may still be a chance of reintro-
ducing the ethical outlook and world-view of the original Jesus into
Christianity.

   This may suggest that I am or could be a liberal-protestant
Christian reformer, of the nineteenth-century type that hoped to use
a rediscovered historical Jesus as the keystone and principle of a New
Reformation. Not so, alas: it is much too late for a conservative reformation. Since 1650 critical thinking has led to a huge knowledge-
explosion in science and history, in technology and in medicine. Not
even the most-assured Islamist really supposes that we could give all
that up and go back to an early-mediaeval technology and world-view.
We are stuck now with our own culturally-mediated form of naturalism, and to an outlook therefore whose religion must be ethics-led
and purely immanent. Roughly, radical humanism, combined with
a mysticism of secondariness or transience: a view that remains close
to the original Jesus, and admires him without any cult of him.
'Authority' is dead, 'revelation' is dead, and the old two-worlds,
mediated kind of religion is dead too, now. So my remaining 'faith'
is purely philosophical, with a dash of loyalty to Jesus, and to the ancient humanitarian strand in our own cultural tradition. Goodbye!

About the Author

on Cupitt is a Life Fellow of Emmanuel College, Cambridge UK—John Harvard's college. As an undergraduate he studied successively natural sciences, theology and philosophy. He was ordained to the Anglican priesthood in 1960, but in 1962 he returned to Cambridge to teach and, since then, has stayed put.

Creative Faith is Cupitt's fiftieth book, and perhaps his most accurate and careful statement of his life's chief purpose, which has been to transform our understanding of life, of religion, and of Christianity in order to reach a faith appropriate for today's world. According to Cupitt, the old faith is all wrong, and it no longer works. It needs to be replaced by a still older faith, which he traces back to the earliest surviving traditions about Jesus.

CPSIA information can be obtained
at www.ICGtesting.com
Printed in the USA
FFOW05n1634060115

9 781598 151534